5S KAIZ
in 90 MINU

For a complete list of Management Books 2000 titles
visit our web-site on http://www.mb2000.com

Other titles in the 'in Ninety Minutes' series are:

25 Management Techniques in 90 Minutes
Active Learning in 90 Minutes
Become a Meeting Anarchist in 90 Minutes
Budgeting in 90 Minutes
Building a Website Using a CMS in 90 Minutes
Credit Control in 90 Minutes
Damn Clients! in 90 Minutes
Effective Media Coverage in 90 Minutes
Faster Promotion in 90 Minutes
Find That Job in 90 Minutes
Forget Debt in 90 Minutes
Funny Business in 90 Minutes
Getting More Visitors to Your Website in 90 Minutes
Learn to Use a PC in 90 Minutes
Networking in 90 Minutes
Payroll in 90 Minutes
Perfect CVs in 90 Minutes
Plan a New Website in 90 Minutes
Practical Negotiating in 90 Minutes
Run a Successful Conference in 90 Minutes
Strengths Coaching in 90 Minutes
Supply Chain in 90 Minutes
Telling People in 90 Minutes
Understand Accounts in 90 Minutes
Understanding Emotional Intelligence in 90 Minutes
Working Together in 90 Minutes

5S
KAIZEN
in
90
Minutes

Andrew Scotchmer

2000

First published in 2008 by Management Books 2000 Ltd
Forge House, Limes Road
Kemble, Cirencester
Gloucestershire, GL7 6AD, UK
Tel: 0044 (0) 1285 771441
Fax: 0044 (0) 1285 771055
Email: info@mb2000.com
Web: www.mb2000.com

British Library Cataloguing in Publication Data is available

ISBN 9781852525477

Acknowledgements

I would like to thank those people without whose help I would never have written this book.

Firstly, my thanks to Stephen Beckett, member of the Chartered Quality Institute, for introducing me to the world of quality management and encouraging me to begin my studies. He set me firmly on a road from which I have never looked back.

I would also like to thank the faculty at Rushmore University who offered me much instruction and encouragement as I worked my way through their unique MBA course. I hope their effective approach to education continues for a long time and that they will provide me with their enlightened thought and advice as I progress towards a Ph.D.

Finally a big thank you to my wife, Yumiko, for the patience she showed each evening and weekend as I laboured away on the manuscript for this book and her continued support and belief in me.

Contents

5S Kaizen Glossary

Definitions of Terms Used in the 5S
Kaizen Approach

Don't feel you need to learn any of these terms by heart; just use the glossary as a reference as you progress through the book. For now, give it a skim and read on. As you develop in your understanding of 5S Kaizen you'll find you'll pick them the terms up soon enough and in your own time. You may also find this list a useful resource and foundation for any other Kaizen books you may choose to read.

5S
The Japanese method for workplace organisation. 5S forms the basis of 5S Kaizen and consists of five separate steps – **Sort**, **Straighten**, **Shine**, **Standardise** and **Sustain**.

Andon
A display board above or at the head of a production line that displays information about the state of production and where problems are occurring. The andon board allows managers to see at a glance what is happening on the shop floor and what areas need some improvement.

Batch-and-Queue
The traditional approach to mass production in opposition to **one-piece-flow**. The main batch-and-queue characteristic is the production of large

units of work that are then placed in a queuing system before moving on to the next process.

Cycle Time　　　A measurement of the time it takes to complete one cycle of work. Ideally this should equal the **takt time** to achieve **one-piece-flow**.

Flow　　　The term given to the movement of work through the workplace without delays or hindrance.

Gemba　　　A Japanese name literally meaning 'right place'. In the context of this book that translates to the workplace or the area under current review.

Gemba Gembutsu　　　An extension to the above term, meaning 'right place, right thing'. Applied to quality improvement it is closely associated to **jidoka** and **root cause analysis,** meaning that when determining the problem, you go and look for yourself at the point of the problem's occurrence.

Heijunka　　　The levelling of work demands by smoothing day-to-day variations to meet the long-term requirements of the customer. Often this involves sequencing work orders as opposed to concentrating on and completing one order before moving on to the next.

Hoshin Kanri　　　'Direction setting' or 'policy deployment'.

Hoshing kanri is a strategic tool used by executive management for identifying critical objectives for the company.

Jidoka

A means of stopping the production line when an error has occurred. This avoids the defective part moving further downstream and causing a costly repair later on, and avoids the defect being repeated in other units. In Toyota they use a chain above each workstation that can be pulled by the operative to stop the line dead – similar to the emergency stop chain that used to be found on trains. Where possible, this mechanism is often found built into the machines that are then able to autodetect any defaults and shut themselves down. The idea began when the founder of Toyota, Ichijiro Toyoda, designed weaving looms that would automatically stop working when a thread broke, thereby avoiding many metres of ruined cloth.

Jishu Kanri

'Autonomous management', referring to the participation of workers in improvement activities as part of their normal daily activities. This is similar to quality circles except for the latter being on a voluntary basis.

Just-in-Time

The system, often referred to as 'lean manufacturing', of providing units of work to departments just in time for their use and in just the right quantities. This is closely associated with **pull** and **kanban**. Just-in-time was developed by Taiichi Ohno when he noticed how supermarket shelves never ran out of items for sale. Instead, just as the shelves were about to become empty, just enough goods to satisfy demand would arrive to replenish the diminishing stocks.

Kaikaku

Often termed a **Kaizen Blitz** or **Rapid Improvement Event** in the west. Kaikaku literally means a sudden revolution, and in our context means the approach of making rapid improvements to a work area. Often used synonymously with **Kaizen.**

Kaizen

Literally meaning 'to change over time (kai) for that which is better (zen)' – or as it is more commonly translated, 'continuous improvement'. Kaizen has become an approach to work that focuses on incremental changes to aid an operations improvement. The word itself is common in Japanese language and conversations. One of its first uses as a way to describe a systematic approach to business improvement was by Masaaki Imai in the mid 1980s.

Kaizen Blitz

See **Kaikaku**.

Kanban

Literally translated, kanban means 'an advertisement board' just like the type we see on the roadside or outside shops. Kanban here describes a method for allowing workers to 'advertise' the fact that they have no work and are in need of more within a **push** production environment.

Lead Time   The total amount of time taken from an order being placed to the goods being received by the customer.

Lean   See the entry for **Toyota Production System**.

Muda   The Japanese word for waste. The removal of waste is central to the **Kaizen** approach and refers to activities that do not add **value**. Taiichi Ohno recognised seven types of waste and others have found more. Ohno's seven wastes include: i) overproduction, ii) excessive movement, iii) repairs/defects, iv) over processing, v) excessive transportation of goods, vi) excessive levels of inventory and vii) waiting times.

Mura   The waste of irregularity in work-flow (see also **Heijunka**).

Muri   The waste caused through the creation of strenuous working conditions for both man and machine.

One-Piece-Flow   The ideal state of operations in a **just-in-time** production environment. One-piece-flow aims to reduce **waste** by focusing on the length of time it takes for one unit to pass through all the production cells. Instead of the **batch-and-queue** method of traditional mass production, one-piece-flow allows workers to concentrate on just one unit at a time before moving it on to the next stage without delay. Thus the work **flows** along the production line.

Poke-Yoke

Literally this Japanese word translates as 'mistake-proofing'. It was developed by Shigeo Shingo and refers to a method for making it hard to make mistakes, and therefore rejects, within the work place. Originally it was called **baka-yoke**, or 'fool-proofing', but Dr Shingo decided to change it to save Japanese sensibilities.

Pull

A central concept in a **just-in-time** production system describing how work travels along the production line. Use of a pull system is evident from how workers downstream use a **kanban** method to 'advertise' the fact that they are ready for more work and the amounts they require. It is opposite to the **push** method, which is usually associated with the traditional view of mass production.

Push

The traditional way of working in mass production environments where one operation will produce as many items as

14

possible and push them downstream, regardless of whether the stations downstream are ready to begin work on the items. Push systems create waste in the form of overproduction, excessive transportation, increased levels of inventory and excessive amounts of waiting time (see **muda**).

Quality Circles   Workers' voluntary involvement in addressing quality matters and implementing changes to improve current processes. These gatherings or meetings consisting of maybe a dozen workers take place at regular intervals with the focus of how to raise the quality of one's output. Similar to **jishu kanri**.

Rapid Improvement   See **Kaikaku**.
Event (RIE)

Root Cause Analysis   A method developed by Kaoru Ishigawa to identify the underlying cause to a problem. His use of a fishbone diagram has become a staple tool for managers around the world.

Staff Suggestion System   A standardised approach for allowing staff at all levels within the organisation to post improvement suggestions. According to Pacale and Athos in their book *The Art of Japanese Management* (1981), the company Mitsushite, who produce electrical equipment under the Panasonic brand, received within one year 25 suggestions per employee –

more than two a month. In a company the size of Mitsushite that comes to many thousands of improvement suggestions each year.

Takt Time

The amount of time for one unit to pass through production in order to meet a customers demand. Often defined by the equation:

$$\frac{\text{Amount of production time available}}{\text{Amount of production needed}}$$

Total Productive Maintenance (TPM)

A means of continually checking and maintaining one's equipment to keep it in optimal working condition so as to reduce equipment downtime and the number of defects.

Toyota Production System (TPS)

The world famous production system developed and applied by Toyota for almost 50 years. TPS is regarded by many as the principle reason for the Toyota company's attaining the position of being the biggest and most profitable vehicle manufacturer in the world at the time of writing.

Value

According to Womac and Jones in their book *Lean Thinking*, value is defined by the customer and provided by the producer. Essentially, value is created in the production process by changing the item on the production line closer to what the customer wants or needs. Any part of the process that does not add to this is classed as waste and should be removed where possible.

Value-Adding Activities

Those activities that add **value** – in other words, those activities that help in giving the customer what they want.

Work Cell

An area of the workplace that contains all the different machines needed to produce a finished item, grouped together in a sequential order. Work cells are based on the **one-piece-flow** production method and are in contrast to the usual shop floor layout that groups together similar machines performing the same function for **batch-and-queue** production.

The Preliminaries

'Those who have changed
the universe have never
done so by changing
officials, but always by
inspiring the people.'

Napoleon Bonaparte

1

Introduction

This book has been written to help your business beat off competition and succeed in an increasingly competitive global market. By providing you with a sustainable, continuous improvement program that is cost-effective, easy to learn and quick to implement, this book will help your company grow and gain that all-important competitive edge so vital for today's organisations. If you are concerned about the future of your company and feel that a new approach to your traditional way of working is needed, this book will ease your worries.

Now, to many that may sound like a very bold statement to make, and I wouldn't be at all surprised to find you sceptical. You've heard it all before, bought the books, read a few, and even implemented some of their suggestions. Yet the very fact that you're reading this book means you have been left feeling a little short-changed if not downright swindled, but trust me on this: I truly believe it is possible for your business to improve if you follow the five-step program discussed within these pages.

The 5S Kaizen method is a time-honoured, tried and tested way of improving operations and delivering bottom-line improvement. It began over 40 years ago in Japan and first came to the attention of the West in the 1980s with the publication of Masaaki Imai's classic book, *Kaizen: The Key to Japan's Competitive Success*. It later gained popularity under the name '**lean manufacturing**', a phrase coined by James

Womac and Daniel Jones in their book, *The Machine That Changed the World,* because of its ability to allow companies to do 'more and more with less and less'.

The company most associated with this method for improvement is Toyota. What made the Toyota Production System so special was the way in which they zealously tackled the problem of inefficient, or wasteful, activities that held up the production process, and the way they managed the supply chain from raw products to the end user. The first of these two areas – tackling inefficiencies and wasteful processes in our work areas – is the principal focus of this book; the book will also deal to a lesser extent with improvements to the supply chain.

Unfortunately, and despite the volumes that have already been written on the subject of Kaizen, many firms, especially here in the West, have found their attempts to implement Kaizen in their organisations leaving much to be desired. Often under the direction of expensive consultants promising miraculous cures that will turn a business around in alarmingly short periods of time, these companies find after a few months that nothing really has changed. The trust placed in the consultants has been abused and in reality, as the old saying goes, all they did was to 'steal your watch and then tell you the time'.

And that is the object of this book – to correct any misunderstanding and to introduce you to authentic, unadulterated Japanese Kaizen. As will hopefully be shown, by following this program, improvement can be realised. Many companies, both big and small, here in the UK and abroad, have benefited from utilising this program for change and have all seen improvements to their systems and processes. Whether you are a member of a large international organisation or a small family-run business you too can reap the benefits this approach to working can bring.

The need for change

As we all know, today's world is moving at a frantic pace. Think of all the changes we have seen in the last two decades, especially in relation to technology. Computers, once a rarity only to be found in a few select offices and operated by a few select individuals, now sit on every desk in every office for everyone to use. Information travels faster today than ever before thanks to the Internet. Once the preserve of military officials and academics, it now connects people and businesses from all over the world, bringing together customer with supplier in a virtual, real-time environment that goes beyond even the wildest expectations of 20 years ago. Indeed, so suddenly has the Internet phenomenon developed, that even Bill Gates the founder of Microsoft and the man synonymous with all things computer related, once famously ignored its potential.

Thanks to the World Wide Web, anybody with a computer and telephone line can become an entrepreneur, and many have, earning themselves millions of pounds for their efforts. From the retailer who uses auction sites such as Ebay and Yahoo, to the small garage owner and mobile hairdresser, all peddle their wares on the virtual network and offer a level of personal service that fills a gap left by the larger organisations. Indeed it is often said that today no-one need leave the comforts of their own homes in order to survive, and with more and more individuals choosing to 'shop on-line' the trend will only increase.

But that is not to say the larger organisations have failed to realise the benefits of 'going virtual'. No major company today can ignore the huge marketing tool the Internet has become, and if exploited in the right manner, that marketing tool can increase sales and revenue exponentially by providing custom from far away countries – countries that would have never

5S Kaizen in 90 Minutes

before been considered as fertile trading ground, or where the costs would have outweighed the rewards. As such, even small locally-based companies are feeling the pressure from the global giants that encroach upon their territory and steal their once loyal custom.

Over the past few decades we have also seen a change in the political landscape of the world. In the late eighties and early nineties the cold war ended and the iron curtain fell. Trade was permitted with once closed off nations and subsequently new markets emerged from the shadows, eager for work and the western produce they had been deprived of for so long. Cheap labour opportunities arose and East European companies jumped at the opportunity to help rebuild their countries' economies, which had been left dissipated by the soviet regime.

On the other side of the planet, in 1978 after the death of Chairman Mao, China began relaxing its old-style communist ideology and opened its borders for trade. Providing cheaper operating costs than could be found in the west, companies from across the globe flocked to her shores and began investing, with the result that many Chinese businesses have grown fat whilst investment in the west has become almost anorexic by comparison. Not waiting to be left behind, South East Asia also promoted the cost benefits of relocating to their countries. Over 2006 and 2007 Vietnam became the fastest growing economy in the world. Thailand too has jumped on board, looking for another income stream besides its tourist standby and India, Cambodia and Malaysia are joining suit.

Management guru Tom Peters once wrote that in the future the most successful companies will be those who 'create themselves anew each day'. With the rise of global markets and increasingly demanding customers, we could argue that the future has arrived. Companies today are facing a constant battle to maintain their market share and keep their once loyal consumers happy. According to business writer Stuart Crainer, 'Currently some 37,000 parent companies control over 200,000 subsidiaries abroad. Some 40% of the total assets of the world's 100 largest companies are already located outside their home countries.' And the situation does not seem to be slowing down.

In a speech given in 2006, Shadow Chancellor George Osborne stated that there is 'no greater challenge' than that of globalisation.

'And the globalisation we have seen is nothing compared to what will come. Over the next ten years, two billion people will join the global economy. Rising out of subsistence poverty, a third of the world's population will begin to connect and trade with the rest of the world.'

Companies of all sizes are finding that in order to become high performance organisations that stay one step ahead of the competition and keep up with shifting customer demands and loyalties, a program of continuous organisational change is necessary.

Unfortunately, for many companies this type of organisational change has proved elusive and hard to carry through. After just weeks of implementing change programmes, old ways of working begin to resurface. Any enthusiasm and commitment that was initially felt begins to wane as 'more pressing matters' take precedence. All in all, change becomes a time-consuming and often expensive exercise that bares little or no fruit. Much of what was promised has not been realised and rather than the far-reaching transformation so eagerly anticipated, all they are left with is a few cosmetic, superficial changes that have little effect on bottom line results.

Often the reasons for such failures and elusiveness lie not in the method itself but the execution. Harvard professor John Kotter listed several common reasons for failure. The reasons he gave included the following:

- Too much complacency
- Lack of communication
- Allowing obstacles to block progress
- Failing to create short term wins
- Neglecting to anchor changes in the company's culture.

However whereas availing ourselves of such knowledge is one thing, knowing how to use it for our development is something else.

The benefits of Kaizen

Kaizen is an everyday Japanese word often translated into English as 'improvement'. Kaizen is actually made up from two words. The first being 'Kai' or 'to change continuously' and the second, 'zen' meaning 'to improve' or 'to get better'. Therefore a more complete understanding of the word Kaizen would be 'to continually make changes to get better'.

Unlike many transformation programs that have come to prominence over the last few decades and that require us to take rapid and large leaps in altering how we work, Kaizen focuses on small incremental change that over time provide an organisation with a sustainable means of delivering improvement. Though it is true that a Kaizen event can be completed in a relatively short period of time, with some exercises taking little more than a few days, its strength lies in setting in place a method for continually looking at and improving what we do. For many it has become a permanent feature of their company's culture – 'the way we do things around here'.

Kaizen has also become an umbrella term for a number of tools and techniques that can be used to implement a continuous improvement program, with 5S being one such technique. Others include 'just-in-time', also referred to as JIT or 'lean manufacturing', and 'quality circles'. Here in the West we tend to separate and pigeonhole these tools, utilising either this one or that as the need demands. In the Far East a more holistic approach is often utilised. This holistic view is the essence of this book and the reason I use the composite term '5S Kaizen'. As Hiroyuki Hirano, author of *The 5 Pillars of the Visible Workplace*, concluded, 'A company that cannot successfully implement the 5S's cannot expect to effectively integrate JIT, re-engineering or any other large-scale change.'

So what is 5S Kaizen?

5S Kaizen is an improvement method that brings together these tools and techniques into a unified whole with 5S forming the base that links all other methods together. For many who have heard of 5S before you may be forgiven for regarding it only as a simple housekeeping exercise. Indeed when some people first learn of the 5S method they find it hard to understand its power and strength as an improvement tool.

As this book will hopefully show, the 5S Kaizen method is much more than a mere housekeeping system. It affords us the opportunity to change the very way we view our work, our working environments and even how we view our roles within our departments. In other words 5S Kaizen allows us to change our whole method of working and develop a culture focused on continuous improvement.

In the Far East, 5S is taken a lot more seriously than here in the West. In Hong Kong, especially, there has been much work carried out in promoting and implementing this method to local businesses. Beginning in the late 1990s, the Hong Kong 5S Association (HK5S) was formed by Professor Sam Ho of the Hong Kong Baptist University and has since gone on to train over 5,000 auditors and staging an annual 5S convention for member businesses. In 2002 they conducted a survey with some interesting results that showed 5S Kaizen was responsible for the following:

- Improved quality
- Improved productivity
- Higher levels of efficiency in the workplace
- Improved safety
- Fewer defects
- A lower number of accidents

- Improved staff morale
- Improved corporate image
- Fewer distractions in the workplace
- Lower operating cost than previously.

To this list we could also add that 5S Kaizen helps companies reduce the level of stock they hold through the introduction of a just-in-time system and by the use of pull systems and kanban symbols, and that it helps staff feel more relaxed and better able to concentrate on their work. Not only that, but 5S Kaizen helps build strong cross-functional teams and helps develop a creative environment for problem-solving and promotes an entrepreneurial culture within departments regarding the development of new improvement ideas. So now that I've whetted your appetite, this is a good time to introduce you briefly to the five steps of the 5S Kaizen approach. Here's a list of the individual steps along with a brief introduction of each.

The Five Steps

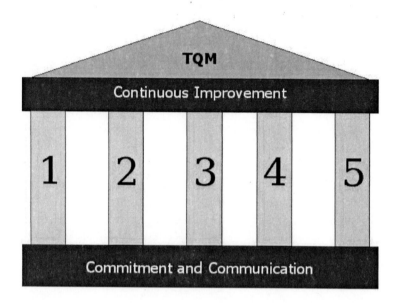

1. Sort

Separate all the necessary items from the unnecessary items in your working environment and removing the latter. Only those items that are in constant use should remain. All other items will only enter the workplace as and when they are needed and not before.

2. Straighten

Arrange and label the necessary production components, tools and equipment in such a way that everyone knows where to find them and where to return them after use. The **'Straighten'** process also looks at improving the flow of work by looking at the layout of the workplace.

3. Shine

Keep everything clean – and that even includes the places no-one can see, like the area under the keyboard or behind the monitor. 'Shine' becomes everyone's responsibility. We are all responsible for keeping the work area tidy and arranged in an orderly fashion.

4. Standardise

This pillar is used to maintain the first three pillars. Once the workplace has been sorted, straightened and shined many people take photographs to act as visual reminders of how the area should remain. These photographs essentially become the standard for the workplace.

5. Sustain

Often thought of as the most difficult pillar to implement, this step focuses on the continuous application of the 5S method and attempts to truly ingrain the concept into our working culture. Many places use accreditation, best practice awards and other techniques to continually keep the importance of the 5 pillars in people's minds.

On the basis of the summary descriptions set out above, it is easy to see how some people mistakenly think of 5S as a simple means to tidy up – albeit in a very organised fashion. However, as I hope this book will show you, this is only a surface description of the process. What lies beneath is a complete way of business improvement and long-term growth that alters and enhances the working environment at both the operational and cultural levels.

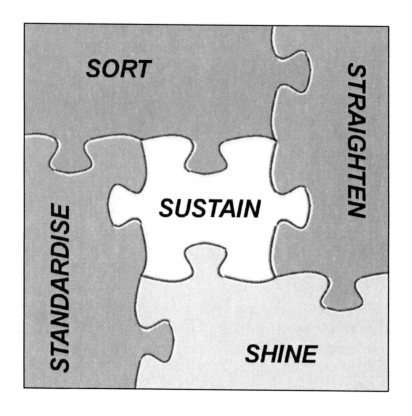

How to use this book

This book can be used both as an introduction to the philosophy and theory of the 5S Kaizen method and as a practical workbook used in implementing a 5S project in your place of work. In fact, within the pages that follow you will find all you need to begin a 5S Kaizen campaign.

As 5S Kaizen is a sequential methodology, it is important that each chapter is read in order. Though some books are written in a style that allows the reader to dip in at random and begin wherever they please, this book is not one of them. The five steps to 5S Kaizen, though presented as separate are in fact dependant upon the others. It is like a large jigsaw with each piece dependant upon the next. In order to begin implementing the second pillar **Straighten**, for example, you must first have completed, or be near to completing, the first pillar **Sort**. To begin implementing the first pillar **Sort**, you should have first laid the proper foundation for sustained improvement. Only by following the prescribed order of events will success be assured. Skip ahead at your peril!

At the end of each chapter you will also find an 'Action Plan' which acts as both a summary of the information you have just learnt and gives you a checklist of points to make it easier for you to understand how the material relates to your own working environment and more importantly how to apply it. As such although this book can be read in just 90 minutes, you may find that to fully comprehend and make successful use of 5S Kaizen, it will take considerably longer.

2

The Japanese Approach

During the 1970s and 1980s something strange seemed to be happening in Japan. Once associated with poor quality imitations of western goods, this country was now shipping high quality affordable items that western manufacturers found hard to beat and that western consumers found hard to resist. What happened has been described by many as a miracle and is the subject of this chapter.

Now I don't want to get bogged down in the specifics of what actually did happen during the intervening years between the end of the second world war and the 1970s, but a little knowledge, I think, will help us gain a better and deeper understanding of where the 5S Kaizen method came from and why it was developed in the first place.

Also there are some who have suggested that the success of the Japanese and the Kaizen approach to work is purely down to their social culture and as such would be hard to replicate in any other country, let alone those of the western hemisphere. I hope that by reading this chapter you may find, as I have, that such a view, although understandable, is fundamentally wrong in its conclusion. If approached correctly, taking into account our own unique cultural settings and ways, the 5S Kaizen approach can work well anywhere in the world, East or West, North or South and help improve that business.

A little history

After the horrors of the Second World War, Japanese industry, like almost everything else in that country, was devastated to the point of almost non-existence. Japan had to literally rebuild itself and that meant spending money, little of which it had. However the Japanese spirit is a proud one and when there is work to be done they willingly jump right in and roll up their sleeves.

Under the influence of America, many Japanese visited the USA to see how their manufacturing industries operated on such large scales. They went to learn about the batch and queue model of mass production which they had read about in their textbooks, and many were impressed by the wonders of the American way, as typified by the work of Henry Ford.

Unfortunately there was one small problem: America is a large country, much larger than Japan, and one with many open spaces where large facilities could be built to satisfy the space required for this method of working. Japan, in contrast, is an archipelago, a series of narrow islands that stretch from the cold north, parallel to Siberia, down to the hot sub-tropics in the pacific. The largest island is Honshu where many of the main cities of Japan, including Tokyo, are to be found. Unfortunately, as it is also located on the site where three tectonic plates meet, this island is very mountainous and the massive population is forced to live, for the most part, on the low plains next to the shoreline. Hence it did not take long for these businessmen to figure out that due to a shortage of space and high land prices, such large plants would be too costly to build in their home countries and they needed instead to find another solution.

The solution came from an unexpected source. Two American management consultants, Dr Joseph Juran and Dr W. Edwards Deming, were at that time offering help and assistance to Japanese businesses by teaching them the importance of, and more importantly the cost savings that could come from, effective quality management. These two Americans have since gone down in management history and such an effect did they have on the fortunes of Japanese industry that both Deming and Juran were awarded the highest honour the Emperor can bestow upon a non-national – The Second Order of the Sacred Treasure.

What these men taught the Japanese was twofold. Firstly there was the message of Deming, who was a highly skilled statistician having gained a Ph.D. in mathematical physics in 1928. His area of expertise followed on from the work of Walter Shewhart, who applied statistical tools to the problem of product variation in manufacturing environments. The use of such tools and techniques lessened the need for product inspection by using sample batches and predictive statistics to determine the probability of there being 'x' number of defects in any given size of order.

Deming and Shewhart's work was very successful in America during the war years and proved its effectiveness at lowering costs and improving quality. However, following the allied victory, American industry was booming, and thoughts of wartime discipline were pushed firmly into the distant past as old ways of working resurfaced. Who needed these frugal thoughts when they had won the war!

Japan on the other hand, and, it must be said, Germany too, were in a position completely opposite to the USA and welcomed the techniques of Deming and Shewhart.

While Deming and Shewhart were concentrating on production processes, Juran's work focused on quality throughout the whole organisation, what he called Company-Wide Quality Management (CWQM), and what is termed today as Total Quality Management (TQM). Again, as with Deming, Juran's work went unrecognised in his home country but found welcoming arms in Japan where his ideas of company-wide quality fitted well with the group-orientated culture of the Japanese.

The Japanese identify very much with the group, more so than they do the individual. It is very much a country where the nail that stands up gets hammered down and where the ideal for many in University is to graduate and become an often anonymous part of one of Japan's large organisations. Throughout their working life they remain committed to their employer, work long hours for the good of the organisation and take far fewer holidays than their western counterparts.

My wife is Japanese and was herself an executive in Tokyo before we married. A friend of hers currently works for a large Japanese company as a computer programmer. To give you an idea of the Japanese working life, her friend is paid more than his western counterpart and receives two bonuses during the year, each totalling nearly twice or three times a normal month's salary. He and his colleagues, despite the downturn of the 1990s (when everyone was saying how Japan was finished), are assured lifetime employment if they do no wrong (such as selling trade secrets – one of the very few things that will get a 'lifer' the sack). However, in return he never takes a holiday. In ten years, he has perhaps taken one, which lasted about four days, and he tells me that his normal working day would start at 7:30 in the morning and very rarely end before 9 o'clock at night. Sometimes he is there until midnight if the work dictates, after which he has a 1½-hour commute back to his bed. The next day he takes things easy and does not arrive at his desk until 08:00, or maybe 08:30 if he *really* wants to take it easy. Some workers have actually been known to skip the commute altogether and just sleep at the office. Try and find that in the west!!!

Where the Japanese concentrated on forming harmonious groups who would work together for long periods, we in the western hemisphere looked at ways to stamp our own marks on projects and developed management theories more focused on top down control than horizontal integration.

In the early 1980s, a their book, *The Art of Japanese Management,* Richard Pascal and Anthony Atmos compared the Japanese approach to management with the American approach. They found that whereas the American manager, Harold Geneen, CEO of ITT, lived up to the traditional western stereotype of being a larger-than-life figure who wanted to stamp his authority on everyone and everything, his Japanese counterpart, Konosuke Matsushita, founder of the Matsushita organisation, tended to blend more homogenously into the company with the intention of becoming just another part of the whole.

Taking this one step further, Matsushita, one of the largest manufacturers of electrical goods in the world, whose products include the Panasonic range, saw the improvement of society as one of their main responsibilities. Konosuke Matsushita stated that although the company had a duty to their shareholders by creating an 'inexhaustible supply of goods', their work was also for the benefit of society by 'creating peace and prosperity throughout the land'. This idea was shared by many Japanese businesses in the 1950s but it is a concept that is only starting to be understood here in the west.

For this reason Juran's message of company-wide quality management, where everyone has a responsibility to the whole, sat well with the already preconditioned Japanese sense of community and fell on responsive ears. Thus did the rise of Japanese manufacturing begin, typified by low-cost, high-quality goods – a reputation that transformed the Japanese economy into one of the richest and most powerful economies in the world, and all within just a few short decades.

The road to quality

Of all the companies in Japan, however, one has become a giant in business improvement circles – Toyota. Like other Japanese companies they too travelled to America and marvelled at its industrial prowess. They also listened with interest to the words of Deming and Juran and learnt much from the Working within Industry project set up during the American occupation. However Toyota didn't just listen and learn. They listened, learnt, applied and improved.

The system developed in the Toyota plants of the 1960s and 1970s was called the Toyota Production System (TPS) and this became a new paradigm in manufacturing methodology, introducing a new and special way of applying the Kaizen principal of continuous improvement to the manufacturing of cars. Indeed so successful was 'the Toyota Way' that many other companies both within and outside the automotive industry began imitating their methods.

In essence TPS is a way of working that combines the Kaizen approach to operational improvement with Deming's 14 managerial points that he devised and published (see opposite). This can simply be boiled down to four main concepts, which may be summarised as follows:

- Removing waste in the system (see the section 'Step one – **Sort**')
- **Standardise** new ways of working
- Involve everybody in the company
- Focus on the 'value stream'

Deming's 14 Points

1. Create consistency of purpose.

2. Adopt the new philosophy.

3. Stop depending upon inspection to achieve quality – rather build quality into the product.

4. Stop awarding contracts purely on the basis of the price tag.

5. Constantly and forever improve every activity in the company.

6. Implement on-the-job training for workers and management.

7. Encourage correct supervision that actively helps people and machines do a better job.

8. Drive out fear based on future speculation and uncertainties.

9. Improve communications between departments, breaking down their separating differences and encourage cross-functional teamwork.

10. Remove all slogans and admonitions regarding ever higher levels of productivity and that intend to push the worker to work harder.

11. Remove standards based on work quotas.

12. Remove the barriers that rob both management and the hourly worker from taking pride in their workmanship.

13. Implement a rigorous re training program.

14. Build programs that rely on teamwork to accomplish the change transformation.

In 1984 Toyota and General Motors (GM) went into partnership, in order to learn from each other the secrets of their successes. Toyota had just purchased their first American plant from GM and wished some 'insider' help to get it off the ground. They agreed to share TPS with GM and would use this plant in Fremont, California almost as a teaching centre. And teach them they did, surpassing all of GM's factories in North America with regard to quality, productivity and cost. Such an impression did this make on GM that they developed their own 'Global Manufacturing System' that was based heavily on the Toyota Way.

Since those days, **'lean manufacturing'** has spread its wings to all sectors of public and private work. One of the latest industries to climb on board the lean revolution is healthcare, where hospitals and other healthcare providers are coming together to work more harmoniously together for the benefit of their patients.

Getting to the root of it all

Vital to the success of a Kaizen program is the need to get to root courses of problems. How many times have we been told of a problem with some operational process only to go to a distant boardroom or office to discuss the matter and determine solutions?

> *'Hey Joe, we have a problem over here with this particular production line!'*
>
> *'Okay we'll all meet all the way over here and discuss it.'*

Much of Kaizen is based on something called Gemba-Gembutsu – literally, right place, right point/time. In his work, Masaaki Imai, founder of the international consultancy practice, The Kaizen Institute, was amazed at how little time we managers in the west actually spend on the shop floor walking the processes. In contrast he would have Japanese managers apologising for only visiting Gemba maybe a dozen or so times each day!

What this close connection to the shopfloor brings is an intimate understanding of the processes so that when problems occur, more practical and often inexpensive solutions can be sought from those who do the work day after day (the real experts). Root causes of the problem can be much more easily determined and rectified when you are actually there looking and talking than if you are sitting in a boardroom, completely disconnected from events as they are happening and with men who would have trouble finding the shop floor never mind walking it.

Kaizen also relies heavily on committed cross-functional teams to drive operational improvements and change. Within a Kaizen/lean company, staff at all levels are positively encouraged to offer improvement suggestions on a regular basis. These changes, if found to be feasible by management, are fully implemented, bringing about a greater sense of ownership and a sense of belonging for the individual or department concerned, and creating an atmosphere of entrepreneurial creativity.

This last point illustrates the way in which Kaizen can bridge the cultural gap between east and west as it provides us with a means not only to develop strong teams and group cultures in our workplace but also to foster the creativity which is needed to satisfy the individualism found in the west.

It's no wonder then that Masaaki Imai referred to Kaizen as the 'the key to Japan's competitive success'.

3

Selling the Vision

Before we start our journey and begin the changes necessary to transform ourselves into truly 21st-century, high-performance organisations, there are a few preliminaries we must work through in order to get the best from the 5S Kaizen exercises that follow. To start with, we must examine our role as leaders.

You may already be a manager, responsible for many people, but that does not mean you will be a good and effective leader. Managers learn how to manage, which requires a different set of skills than those required of a leader. Managers know about meeting deadlines, organising labour and resources to meet delivery, ensuring quality to within agreed customer specifications, budgeting, recruitment, and a host of other, very precise and goal-orientated tools.

Leaders on the other hand know about motivation, and seeing clearly the future state and how to get there. They are effective communicators and can rally the troops to unprecedented levels of activity and commitment when necessary. Leaders are inspiring visionaries with their sights set firmly on the future long-term goals, the 'big picture,' whereas Managers tend to focus on the specifics of day-to-day, 'getting the job done,' activity and tend not to stray too far from the short-term objectives of the company.

In his book *Managing on the Edge*, Richard Pascal stated that 'Managers do things right, while leaders do the right thing'.

Managers are by training methodical and creatures of habit, whereas leaders on the other hand are revolutionary and free from traditional ways of working. Such freedom allows leaders to see what could be rather than what is. That is not to say that both qualities cannot co-exist but understanding these differences is necessary if we want to be able to motivate change from within. We must know when to be the manager and when the leader in order to ensure that transformational change is delivered to agreed time scales, with the proper administration yet never loosing sight of the big picture, the future state we are all striving for.

Types of leadership

Over the last few decades there have been many attempts to describe what qualities make for effective leadership, with many books being published on the subject. So much has been said that Joseph Boyett, author of *The Guru Guide*, spoke of the subject as being 'the most popular topic in all of business literature'. He went on to say that 'Every business guru, it seems, has written at least one book and/or collection of articles on [leadersip].' Though the full range of ideas covered is well beyond the scope of this book, it may be worth reviewing some thoughts that have come to prominence and acceptance over the last decade or so.

A leader is commonly regarded as someone with a desire to lead, displaying an entrepreneurial spirit not afraid to stand up and be counted and to take risks if the rewards are great enough. However, as Peter Drucker once observed, such traits are not essential to be a leader.

*'Among the most effective leaders I have encountered and worked with in a half century, some locked themselves into their offices and others were ultra gregarious. Some (though not many) were 'nice guys' and others were stern disciplinarians... The one and only personality the effective ones I have encountered did have in common was something they did **not** have: they had little or no 'charisma' and little use either for the term or for what it signifies.'*

Leaders are appointed rather than promoted and as such one defining attribute of a leader is that he has followers. These followers have been described as those who follow willingly either through identifying with the leader or with the message. Either way followers must feel some kind of emotional attachment without which change could not happen. This attachment is borne not from charisma and charming your staff into action, but by building relationships based upon a solid, shared understanding of each other's needs.

To help build an emotional connection it helps to simplify your message. This is one reason that 5S Kaizen is so popular and has received so much interest – because at its heart is a common-sense simple message. At this stage of the game, rather than focusing on the minor details and getting into a position popularly known as 'paralysis by analysis', think in the round. Think and communicate the big picture and you will probably find that solutions to the finer points will be forthcoming from those who know best. Spice your vision with a story to create the picture of the future state in people's minds, and finally never let a cool reception deter you or sway you from your course. If you initially find only a handful of interested participants, work with them, for as social anthropologist Margaret Mead once said, 'Never doubt that a small group of thoughtful, committed citizens can change the world. Indeed, it is the only thing that ever has.'

Developing your vision

From the above, you may have realised that the first step in leadership is to create a crystal clear vision of a future state which you can then communicate to others. According to Theodore Hesburgh, President of the Notre Dame University,

'The very essence of leadership is that you have to have a vision. It's got to be a vision you articulate clearly and forcefully on every occasion.'

I can only talk in general terms here as I don't know your organisation, nor do I know the level of support that may or may not exist in your company for this type of transformational change. You may be a lone radical who has spotted an opportunity for improvement and wants to do something about it (in which case you already possess the character of a leader) or you may be reading this under instruction from those above who have an interest in this approach but little time to devote to study. Either way I hope this chapter will be useful in helping you kick start your 5S Kaizen change program.

Let me start by saying that when I talk of a vision, I am not referring to some vague blue-sky ideal that sounds good and enticing but bares little or no relevance to the practicalities of getting the job done or to the external pressures your market sector is facing. On the contrary, the term as it is used here means a picture of a future way of working that is both attainable in the short term and sustainable for future growth. To be effective you must be basing your foresight on a thorough understanding of where you are now, knowledge of best practise within your industry, and the differences that lie between. Your vision must be realistic and practical in order to win support.

Communicating the change

The reason leadership skills are so important to the 5S Kaizen way is that we are about to undertake a program of transformational change. I use the word transformational to describe the far-reaching effects the 5S Kaizen approach to workplace reorganisation can have once the momentum gets going. However before that momentum begins we may find a few hurdles to overcome along the way and that is what we will now consider as we discuss how to get your message out there and accepted – in other words, how to sell your vision.

According to Harvard professor John Kotter, communication is one of the main reasons change endeavours fail. Paul Slone reiterated this view in his book, *The Leaders Guide to Lateral Thinking Skills,* when he stated that 'resting on your laurels is a sure way to slide into complacency and defeat at the hands of your competitor.' Change management also remains one of the most misunderstood of disciplines and as such has caused many companies to hesitate before committing to a program of organisation-wide transformation – a hesitation that could cost valuable time in rapidly changing, globally competitive markets. According to Stuart Crainer, 'Change is now endemic in the business world...Change is a worldwide issue.'

At its most basic level, organisational change has been described as 'moving from one state to another'. Though on the surface this may sound a simple task to manage, experience and research have shown it to be more problematic than this statement implies.

One of the problems faced in getting from the old state to the new, and in communicating the future vision, is the fact that the new state only exists as an ideal; it does not exist in any tangible form in the present moment. This means that besides simply changing *how* we work, we must also account for *why*

50

we work. Matrix Research and Consultancy commented on these deeper aspects of change in their 2006 white paper, *What is Transformational Change,* by reasoning that 'the objective of transformational change is to not only influence processes, but to change mindsets, cultures, activities and organisational power bases.'

Though 5S Kaizen is very much process-orientated, to successfully implement and sustain an endeavour we also need to change people's mindsets – their attitude to their working environments, the work they do, and their roles within the company. For this reason 5S Kaizen can be described as a *transformational* change – a change that alters, either incrementally or over the course of a few days or weeks, every business practice we and our organisation is involved in. We need to critically look at our work and be constantly questioning the motives for working the way we do. For this to happen, however, such a change towards the 5S Kaizen method must first be communicated, followers identified, short-term wins realised and, if we are at a middle managers level or below, then we need to gain commitment from the top.

Overcoming the hurdles

People by their nature like stability. It brings with it security and comfort and gives people an anchor to cling to. Unfortunately from our standpoint it also brings about complacency and a general feeling of apathy and a disbelief that things are really as bad as they seem. It's not uncommon to hear people talk of times when things were much worse and how 'they all pulled through just fine back then so why all the fuss now?' It is as though there is disbelief in the reasons for change and on occasions many will believe it is just a cover-up for some deeper agenda those upstairs don't what to admit to – like job cuts to save money.

Such response is common and, as the saying goes, being forewarned is forearmed, so consider yourself warned because it will happen to one degree or another when you first communicate your change vision.

Elizabeth Kubler-Ross was a Swiss doctor who cared for the dying. She developed a theory regarding grief after many years' experience consoling the relatives of her patients. The 'grief cycle' as it has become known is also applicable to the emotions involved in organisational change and a diagram of it is printed on page 54.

During this cycle people and groups move through different stages that vary between active and passive emotions. Denial (it can't be) turns to anger (why me?). Therefore by understanding the different stages a person goes through when some change occurs, this helps us to plan our approach to change and we can better prepare others and ourselves for what is to come. That is not to say everyone will go through all these emotions. Some individuals may jump straight on board and these should be rallied and used as you further communicate your vision, but others, possibly even the majority, will experience some if not all of these feelings during the course of change.

When looking at the graph, one thing we must watch out for and defuse where possible is groups or individuals getting stuck at any one stage. The Kubler-Ross theory is that each stage is passed through in order until the final acceptance of the change sinks in. However, for many reasons blockages can occur and stop the progression. Sometimes the cycle has been known to go back and repeat a stage. The best thing to do in such a situation is to clearly communicate your intent and work closely with those who showed early interest. Develop your future change agents, educating them in the 5S Kaizen way and give them assignments that offer short-term, quick rewards which can be used as selling points during the next round of talks. Then gradually, one-by-one, as people progress at their own pace through the chart opposite and hear of the good news from other departments about the effects of the 5S Kaizen change, groups will form and take a hold of the new approach, all the time lessening the influence, resolve and the power of the dissenters.

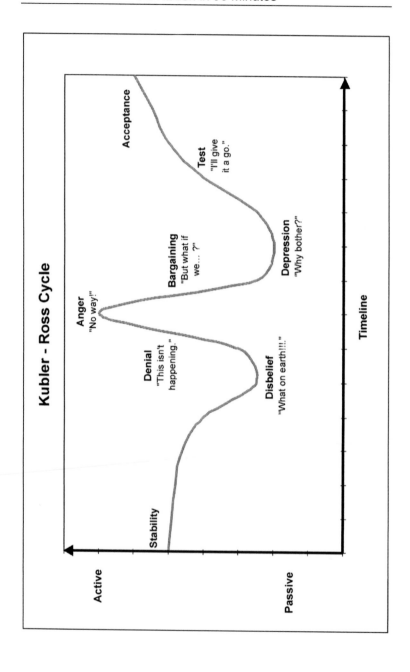

Short-term wins for long-term growth

When discussing short-term wins, there is nothing as important as making the win visible to all and identifying them with the change initiative. When the short-term win is seen to be directly related to (and because of) the change program, an increase in excitement and momentum towards further changes can be generated. John Kotter says that this is achieved by 'planning for results instead of praying for them'. Don't just rely on short-term gimmicks to fuel your change initiative; actually plan for real results that will silence the critics and build momentum. When you identify people coming on board, at the 'testing' phase of the grief cycle, assign them to a group carrying out the change; give them a small task from the repertoire of tools you will learn. Actually get them involved in the change as early as possible to avoid them slipping back to the depressing talk of the doubters. However, one should also be aware that claiming victory regarding these wins too soon, or to an excessive extent, can be damaging to the overall mission and derail the whole program of change.

Concentrating too much on the win can lead to a false sense of security and lead many to feel that the long-term objective of change has been realised. To counter such a climate developing, leaders must constantly push for greater change and impose even stricter targets in the future. In other words leaders must consolidate the victories and use them to generate greater changes, by maintaining a strong focus on the purpose of the change and never letting slip the overriding vision that fuels all subsequent change action.

Unfortunately, altering the perception and behaviour of a company is only one part of the change initiative, and one can find one's hard work undermined unless the changes becomes part of the everyday life of the organisation. The changes must permeate throughout and ingrain themselves into the very culture of the company if they are to remain. Fortunately 5S Kaizen accounts for this need during its final step, **Sustain**, as we will see later.

The 5S Kaizen

'It takes a lot of courage to release the familiar and seemingly secure, to embrace the new. But there is no real security in what is no longer meaningful. There is more security in the adventurous and exciting, for in movement there is life, and in change there is power.'

Alan Cohen

4

Sort

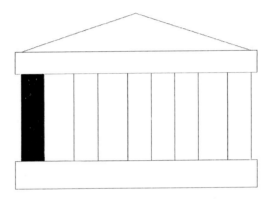

As mentioned previously, **Sort** is the first stage in a 5S Kaizen program and is basically concerned with the removal of waste, or non-value adding items, from a work area. Removing waste is the central underlying principle of 5S Kaizen, and by removing it, **Sort** helps us to create a clutter free efficient workplace where any problems can be immediately identified and resolved and people feel less stressed and more in control.

However, as simple as removing waste may sound, it is surprising how many people struggle to distinguish between what is necessary and what can be removed. It is as if, as a nation of hoarders, we find it difficult to throw away unwanted items, always believing what is thrown out today will be needed again tomorrow.

As a result, the amount of waste that builds up can, in some instances, be enormous. Whether you work in an office or a workshop, unused items can be found stacked high on shelves, in cupboards and in corners. Broken equipment that should have been discarded weeks, months or even years ago remains to collect dust in unseen locations – occupying space that could be utilised for something far more productive. In fact one company that was planning an expensive relocation due to insufficient space found, after a 5S Kaizen program, that they had more than enough once space in their current facilities after unused items had been removed and they had reorganised what remained. If space is at a premium in your place of work, then implementing **Sort** may bring some surprising results and you may just find that your once dingy and claustrophobic environment suddenly becomes a much more comfortable place in which to work.

Defining waste

Before we actually begin implementing **Sort** and because the removal of all waste is so central to this method, it may be useful to digress a little and clarify just what we mean by the term 'waste'.

In Japan there are three varieties of waste – **mura, muri,** and **muda**, often called the 'three mu's'. Of these, the most important is muda, but before we move on to an examination of this main pillar of waste, I will first offer a brief introduction to the first two, **mura** and **muri**.

Mura

Mura is the waste caused by an irregular workflow. Often this can be caused by processes taking longer to complete than was originally determined and designed for. As an example, an operator or process that takes considerably longer than expected holds up the whole internal supply chain and forces the flow of work to be measured by the slowest of procedures. Often this irregularity can be overcome quite simply once it is identified.

For example, a new starter would not be able to work at the same rate as an experienced operator. Therefore, until training has been completed, and time is afforded the individual to settle in and improve, such irregularities can only be expected. To many that may sound like common sense, but the number of firms that offer little or no training and just expect the individual to pick up the job quickly and work at full steam in a short space of time is surprisingly large. Providing adequate training, paced to match the new person's learning curve, and offering a mentor to work alongside them to ensure work continues as usual and as planned for, will reduce **mura** to acceptable limits.

Muri

Muri concerns wastes associated with overly strenuous work. This applies equally to both workers and machinery. In the above example of the new starter, if little or no training is given to the new recruit then his work will be strenuous leading, as mentioned to **mura**. Even for older hands, asking them to perform under strenuous conditions can lead to difficulties. These difficulties can end up costing the company in days off due to illness or worse if some medical intervention was required. Hence ensuring our workplace is free from strenuous working conditions – **muri** – can help our staff become happier in their work and save the company from extra costs.

With regard to machinery, overproduction can cause strain and lead to problems including extended periods of downtime. Depending on the type of machinery involved this can be expensive, necessitating either a new machine being bought or specialist service engineers being called in. More of this form of waste will be discussed during the **Shine** stage of 5S Kaizen implementation.

Understanding muda

When talking of waste with regard to a Kaizen implementation project, there is one man whose name is synonymous with the subject – Taiichi Ohno. No book on the subject of 5S Kaizen would be complete without some discussion of his theories. Whilst working at Toyota, Taiichi Ohno developed a list of seven types of waste that we should all watch out for when performing a 5S Kaizen activity. He believed that these wastes contributed the most to a company's inefficiencies and he became famous in Toyota as a zealot for rooting out wasteful activities.

On many occasions Ohno would ask junior managers to stand in one spot on the shop floor for hours at a time. He even went to the extreme of drawing a chalk circle on the floor, which they were not to step outside of until he came to collect them. Though extreme, many who took part in this exercise came to a full understanding of the processes they were observing as well as where the inefficiencies and problems in the production cycle surfaced.

Though these are often referred to collectively as '**Ohno's 7 wastes**' it should be noted that he never assumed that this was a definitive list. Since his writing, others have added different wastes as they were observed, the most common being the waste of unused human creativity or potential; indeed you too may find other types of waste as you progress in your knowledge and through your practical experience.

As waste elimination is so important to a 5S Kaizen project's success and so central to its overall philosophy, you will probably refer to this list throughout your exercises, not just during the **Sort** stage, and for this reason a thorough understanding of these 7 wastes should be attained.

Though the main form of waste we are concerned with during the **Sort** stage is that of excessive inventory we will use this opportunity to introduce all the seven types and so lay a foundation for what will come. Ohno's 7 areas of waste are as follows:

Ohno's 7 Wastes

1. **Waste of Over production**

2. **Waste of Inventory**

3. **Waste due to Rejects and Repairs**

4. **Waste of Excessive Motions**

5. **Waste of Over Production**

6. **Waste of Waiting**

7. **Waste of Transportation**

Generally speaking, we can describe waste as all activities and items related to an activity that does not add value. Each activity in your company, whether in the office processing information, or on the shopfloor, either contributes to or detracts from the addition of value. By removing waste we focus on those activities that detract from the addition of value and thus leave only what is necessary. By such elimination of non-value adding activities, the process becomes more efficient in satisfying customer demands.

Overproduction and Inventory

The waste, or **muda**, of overproduction occurs when equipment is left to run even when the immediate order requirements have been met. Why is this a waste? Overproduction leads to an increase in inventory, another of Ohno's wastes. This inventory then needs storage space and perhaps care to avoid any deterioration in quality. Each of these activities do not add value to the customer. In another company that practiced 5S Kaizen, they found that their total obsolete inventory added up to several years worth of stock. Thought of in monetary terms, that would total a far from acceptable amount to have just lying around and what has been called 'the hidden company'. Controlling overproduction and preparing work schedules to handle only the immediate requirements of an order reduces the chances of creating waste.

Another consequence of producing more than what is immediately needed is the added cost of raw materials and the manpower involved in their care and transportation. Why empty your goods-in warehouse, only to pay for its restocking, when half if not more can be found sitting on pallets waiting to be processed or to be scrapped at a later date? Why pay someone for an activity that is not necessary? Yet day after day, week after week, year after year, companies waste millions in paying staff for work that may be later scrapped and on supplies that should not have been used in the first place. Would it not be more prudent to employ those individuals in more value-adding activities or to only order the raw material when it is needed and then only in the amounts needed?

Of all the seven wastes that Taiichi Ohno identified and listed, the waste of overproduction is the worst kind. Indeed to many it is thought of as being worse than that of underproduction. Overproduction leads to all kinds of other wastes. Its complete removal should be one of our main priorities during our 5S Kaizen event.

Other costs involved with excess inventory include the procurement and maintenance of equipment, and the care and transportation of the stock. Forklift trucks, warehouse space, conveyor-belt systems are all bought and installed for the simple purpose of caring for inventory – not to mention the administrative duties required to log the amounts and the personnel required to fill these posts.

Repair and Rejects

Besides overproduction and inventory, Ohno listed repairs and rejects as a form of waste. Why include repairs as a waste? Surely rejects are waste but once repaired...?

Rejects are waste because of the time and cost of materials used in their manufacture – even if the fault was spotted halfway through the manufacturing cycle. Sometimes these costs cannot be recovered and the reject is scrapped. Other times, however, the rejects can be repaired and many companies employ workshops for that exact reason.

Unfortunately the process of repair is itself costly, and can lead to a net loss on the item concerned, especially if we are working to low profit margins. Either way, scrap or repair, it costs! Using 5S Kaizen methods can help reduce incidences of such waste and lower the costs associated with scrapping or repairing work.

The waste of motion

'**Unproductive motion**' refers to those movements that are unrelated to the task at hand and cause extra time to be introduced to a straightforward procedure. In studies it has been discovered that the actual motion required to complete a task is minimal compared to the motion actually involved. Each non-value adding action takes extra time to perform and thus increases the lead-time of the production cycle. How often do we find that essential everyday items of equipment are inappropriately located, requiring us to walk or move more than is truly necessary? As an example I once worked in an office and as part of my duties needed to use the printer several times a day. Unfortunately for me the printer was situated in another office that was down the corridor and two doors on the right. Why was there no printer in my office I hear you ask? The owners of the company believed the cost of giving me my own printer was prohibitive when I could walk. What they hadn't accounted for was the time they were paying me to do just that – walk between two offices several times a day.

The waste of processing

When a piece of work or information moves along from one process to another, it is expected that at each stage value will be added. As was described in chapter 1, 'value' for these purposes describes any activity that helps move the item on to the next stage as quickly as possible whilst meeting customer requirements. Each stage along the line works to the requirements necessary before moving the item on to the next stage. Unfortunately on many occasions what really happens is that either the requirements are not met first time, resulting in rework, or too much 'polishing' takes place that is unnecessary. Both create waste and do not add value.

Another example of over-processing is employing the latest equipment when the older version still has many uses and years of life left in it. Often the improvements to the new model are superficial in nature and do not add value, or its new functionality is such that, for the job it is employed to carry out, many of the new improvements will never be utilised.

The waste in waiting

How often do we find ourselves in a lengthy queue feeling we are just wasting our time. Whether in a bank, a shop or an airport, we naturally hate having to wait in line unnecessarily when there are so many things we could be doing. Yet why is it we so readily accept queues in the workplace with large batches of work in progress lying idle in store rooms and pallet loads on the shop floor just waiting until the next process catches up?

Removing waiting time and working with smaller batch sizes by the introduction of a JIT system reduces the waste of waiting.

Transportation

Whereas '**waste of movement**' relates to personnel, the '**waste of transportation**' refers to work. Excessive transportation, moving products from one end of the factory to the other, from storage to shopfloor and back again, is another waste we need to completely eradicate. Forklift trucks moving to and fro transporting unneeded items unnecessarily is a waste of resources and time.

When we begin to understand the different types of wastes listed here, not to mention the ones you may discover in your own work, we begin to notice muda everywhere. It almost becomes an obsession and you will not be able to rest until you have eradicated it completely.

Implementing Sort

Though the removal of all waste is central to the 5S Kaizen approach, during the **Sort** stage we are mostly concerned with clearing away the waste of excessive inventory – in other words, those items of equipment and work in progress that are unused, broken or just not needed but that, for one reason or another, are still hanging round our immediate environment. When implementing **Sort**, ask yourself the following questions:

- Do I really need these items for the current task in hand?
- How many of these items do I really need?
- By having this item in my immediate workspace, does it really improve my productivity and efficiency?
- When did I last use this piece of equipment?
- When will I next use this piece of equipment?

However, just asking these questions is not enough, and just as knowledge without action is of little use then just being aware of the problem is not in itself a solution. Some action on our part is required if we want to benefit from this change program – but what action and how can we best implement it?

First off, unless your company is small enough, an organisation-wide, simultaneous 5S Kaizen program may well be impractical. Instead, we should first locate a suitable area to start implementation. This area can be determined through a staff suggestion system, or if size and time permit, by walking the shopfloor and offices and physically looking. Another alternative is to run two 5S Kaizen campaigns together, one in the offices and one on the shopfloor, with teams from each area observing the other.

One benefit of beginning small is that it allows for quick and dirty results that can be promptly 'advertised' throughout the company and used to encourage others to get involved. This benefit is especially true if you have doubters within your ranks who, unless brought on board quickly, could jeopardise the whole program of change. Offering some quick improvements that are clearly visible for all to see can help even the most hardline, anti-Kaizen individual to join in the fun.

One is best

To help those people who find throwing away old items of equipment, or find it difficult in distinguishing just what is needed from what is not, 5S Kaizen uses the **'one-is-best'** rule. The reasons some people find difficulty in identifying and dealing with waste may be as numerous as the amounts of waste found. Sentimental attachment or the attachment to an object's potential use all get in the way of proper implementation of Sort.

For these reasons many 5S Kaizen projects use teams from other work areas to carry out the initial inspection of an area and offer their suggestions. These teams, who have no sentimental attachment to the environment, can look more clinically and bring a level of objectivity to the exercise that others more familiar with the area could not. In other words they bring 'a fresh pair of eyes' to the problem of waste identification and removal.

The **'one is best'** rule means exactly what it says – wherever possible there should only be one of every item left in the workplace. Whether you work with a biro, a post-it pad, or a spanner, ask yourself 'how many do I really need to complete my task?' Granted biro pens come in various colours as spanners come in various sizes, but how many of each colour and size are needed? I know that when I worked in one office I had countless pens of various colours, some of which I never needed – green for example. When totalled up, these amounted to nearly half a month's stationary order for pens. Not only pens but erasers, pencils, post-it note pads and half filled jotters were all found within my drawers amongst an array of smaller items. Again, how many do we really need at any one time? How many jotters can we scribble on at once? How many post-it notes do we really make in a day? I'll leave you to answer these questions yourself.

So for those who struggle to decide what should be kept and what should be removed think of the 'one is best' rule for everything and remove all repeated items, the pens back to the stationary cupboard and the spanners back to the tool box – unless, of course, there is an absolute reason for having two of them in the work area.

As a final thought on the 'one is best' rule, in his book *The Toyota Way*, Jeff Liker observed that Toyota have a policy that all reports and documents should fit on one side of an A3 sheet of paper. The reason was both practical (it was the largest size that would fit in the fax machines) and efficient – only the facts are listed and one does not have to get bogged down in detail. If you need detail you ring up and enquire.

One is Best

- **One Pen**
- **One note book**
- **One standard operating procedure**
- **One set of tools**
- **One ream of printer paper**
- **One hour maximum where possible on the length of meetings!**

Red Tagging

Now that we have only one of everything in the workplace we can begin to look more critically at what we have remaining. Obviously, the next items to discard are the broken objects. That printer in the corner that has never worked since last year needs to go, and go to the skip! I can never understand why we often see broken equipment in our workplace taking up valuable space whilst at the same time complain about how short of space we are and how we need a larger area in which to work. The same can be said for unused items that are lying around because no-one has returned them to their rightful 'homes' after finishing the task they were used for.

To easily identify broken or unused equipment 5S Kaizen uses '**Red Tags**'. These are simply pieces of paper, traditionally coloured red, which are attached to items for removal. On the next page is an example of a red-tag that can be used in your exercise. Do you notice the areas to write where the item came from and where it should be sent? This is to allow the tracking of items during the **Sort** exercise and to calculate a monetary value for those items that are scrapped. After the event these tags are saved and sent to the event leader for analysis.

Other items identified through the use of the red tags are those items of work that we are not immediately working on. Due to overproduction, the workplace can very easily become cluttered. If you find during your **Sort** exercise that you have items of work in your immediate environment that are not immediately needed then they should be removed with instructions to return to sender.

RED TAG

NAME:..

ITEM:..

DEPT:..

DATE:..

REASON & ACTION:

And what are the receivers of these unneeded items to do when they see their own work areas becoming cluttered due to the sheer volume of the work returned? Hopefully they will learn not to overproduce by such large amounts in the future!

To further simplify the decision as to what should go or what items need to stay, 5S Kaizen uses 'red-tag areas' where items selected for removal are stored for an agreed period of time to further determine their level of usage; usually two weeks or so. If the items in question have remained unused in that time, they can then be confidently removed to a suitable location where they will not be cluttering up the work area. Items that have been used can be positioned closer to hand; how close will depend on the number of times they were needed.

Now that we have removed all unnecessary, broken or replicated items in our workplace we find that what was once a cluttered and claustrophobic environment is now comfortable and airy. However let's not celebrate too soon. Remember, Sort is only the first of 5 steps in the 5S Kaizen program. What we now need to do is to move swiftly on to the second stage – **Straighten**.

Action Plan

The Sorting stage is the first stage of a 5S Kaizen programme of change. Its main focus is the removal of all wastes associated with excessive unnecessary items in our workplace whether they be broken equipment, duplicated equipment, work-in-progress or anything that is not needed for the immediate job at hand.

- Identify an area to begin your 5S Kaizen campaign.

- One of the best ways to begin is through a red-tagging exercise.

- Introduce your staff to red-tagging and Ohno's wastes.

- Remember the one-is-best rule when determining an item's usefulness.

- Broken items can be scrapped straight away.

- Determine a course of action for the red-tagged items.

- Set up a red-tag area to store items removed from the work area.

- Document red-tagged items and those that were scrapped.

$\overline{\underline{5}}$

Straighten

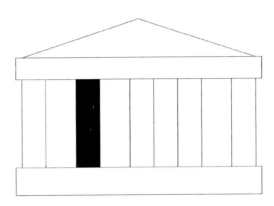

We now have a working environment that is free from all the unnecessary items and the broken equipment and we may be beginning to realise how much free space we have been left with. The job of this stage, **Straighten**, is to make sure that what is remaining is placed in such a way to ease the flow of work in our areas and that the items removed are suitably relocated, loaned out or thrown away – if they haven't already.

That is why I said in the introduction that 5S Kaizen is a sequential approach, because what would be the use of straightening unused and unnecessary items? Until all of the sorting has been done, there is no point in applying **Straighten**. If you failed to heed my advice or you have begun this book by dipping in here and there and did not read my warning, go back to the beginning and read from page one!

Whereas **Sort** was interested in the waste of excessive

inventory, **Straighten** is more concerned with the other six types of waste and tries to eliminate excessive movement, waiting, searching, walking, excessive transportation, number of defects, the need for repair and a host of other wasteful activities.

Making it obvious

One highly effective way of reducing these types of waste is through the use of visual management. This means that everything in the work area is clearly identifiable regarding what and where it is. If a new starter was to begin at your place of work tomorrow and you asked him or her to bring you a much needed piece of equipment how long would it take for them to find it without assistance? If the answer is 'quite some time', then you must ask how efficient your workplace truly is. Remember in **Sort** we discussed muri, the waste caused through stress in the workplace? Well, this is an instance, and making your departments very visual helps to combat this waste and reduce the time it takes for anyone, not just the new starters, to find what they need.

> **Visual Management:**
>
> **The technique of providing information and instruction about the elements of a job in a clearly visible manner so that the worker can maximise his productivity.**
>
> **Massaki Imai**

One of the first steps we can take in making our work areas visual is to label everything and assign each piece of equipment to a specific storage space, again clearly labelled as to its contents. Some I have known even use photographs of the cupboard or cabinet contents and stick them to the doors. Others have removed the doors altogether. We may already think that our working environments and departments are very clear as far as labelling is concerned, but are they really?

What's behind that door over there? A storeroom, maybe a meeting room, possibly the staff rest room? What's in that cupboard over there in the corner? Is it for keeping tools safe, storing stationary, or possibly first aid equipment? Can I tell at a glance without even opening the doors to find out? Talking of first aid, who are our trained first aiders? Do they wear a jacket or a badge or a different coloured hat to identify themselves and make them prominent as being trained if we hurt ourselves? Or do we have to walk around bleeding all over the place until we find one? Sure you have the names of appointed first aiders on a list over on the notice board, but are they up to date or has it been covered with other, more recent notices? For a new starter on their first day, such information should be clear and unambiguous, allowing them, as well as the more experienced, to concentrate fully on what they are doing.

Another useful visible management technique is the use of shadow boards. Tools are mounted on these boards (for example using hooks) and behind each tool is pasted a silhouette of the tool. Whenever the 'shadow' can be seen we know the tool is in use. You may have seen them at your local garage when you take your car in for a service, or you may even have one in your own garage at home. The tools on these boards should also be arranged in order of size if necessary to aid the quick retrieval of a needed item. In other words what we are trying to do is make the time it takes to find anything as minimal as possible. It's called the **30-second rule** – if you can't find something in 30 seconds, it's taking you too long.

Basically, visual controls are anything that communicates something to us with only a glance. There is an old saying that a picture speaks a thousand words and that is exactly the meaning behind this. So when you design your visual control system think carefully about the message you want to communicate and the best and easiest way to go about it. As an example, are your walkways clearly identified and free from clutter? If there is no indication of where a walkway ends and the workplace begins we cannot complain if items are left in areas where people can trip over them or for some reason they become damaged. Using paint or brightly coloured tape, mark lines on the floor and make it a ruling that nothing, and I mean absolutely nothing, is to be left within those lines, within the designated walkway.

Another aim of visual management is to make the identification of errors easy. In fact so easy should it be that errors stand out like a sore thumb. Often we like to brush problems out of sight, especially if they're small. This is in direct opposition to the principle of making your workplace visual, and the 5S Kaizen way in general. Problems are to be celebrated and seen as an opportunity to improve. By making them obvious, this helps us to make many improvements.

Associated with this is the practice know as '**poke-yoke**', or mistake proofing. Poke yoke is a means of achieving zero-defects. You may have heard how Japanese companies can go many weeks and months without producing any rejects – this is how they do it. One often-used example of a poke-yoke system is when machines are designed to stop whenever something is wrong. The Japanese call this ability '**jidoka**' and one of the first instances appeared in the Toyota company.

Before Toyota made vehicles they manufactured weaving looms. One of their popular models had the ability to switch itself off whenever a single thread snapped. Before this facility was introduced, the broken thread would have gone unnoticed with the only indication being reams of ruined cloth. Therefore, by switching off the machine automatically whenever an error occurred, this saved the company money in wasted material. It also acted as a visible symbol saying, 'fix me'. Since then such practices have carried over into their automotive manufacturing plants, with machines that shut down or switch to standby whenever a fault is detected. They also have pull-chains installed for operators like on the old fashioned trains. Whenever an operator notices something wrong they pull the chain and stop the line. A large flashing light over the work area usually accompanies this.

I recall hearing an account of a European business that asked a Japanese engineering firm to supply them with parts. The European firm insisted they saw the rejects and specified a percentage they deemed acceptable. The Japanese agreed though seemed somewhat puzzled and set to work.

A few months later the first shipment of goods arrived accompanied by two reps from the Japanese firm. They showed their goods and when displaying the rejects asked politely, like all good Japanese do, why the Europeans wanted rejects. Of course the European firm started to explain their reasons: to find out if there were any common problems with the manufacturing process and if there were problems, then to perhaps offer some suggestions and assistance in correcting them or maybe altering the design.

Unfortunately and to their embarrassment, they had not listened carefully to the words of the Japanese; or maybe it was a case of the meaning being lost in translation. What the Japanese had asked was 'Why do you want rejects?' They had set up and run a separate line just to cater for making rejects in line with the customer requirements.

Using poke-yoke through the installation of jidoka devices on our machines and visual management systems makes the production of rejects hard, leading eventually to error-free production.

Straightening the flow

Besides making the workplace very visual so that time wasted looking for items and errors is reduced, **Straighten** also looks at ways to improve the flow of work between processes. As its name suggests, flow refers to the unhindered movement of parts between stations. Often, in longstanding environments, the use of space in work areas is planned simply. If a new starter needs a desk, and there is space over there, then that's were the desk goes, regardless of the work they are being hired to do or how their work fits into other activities within the department. Hence we find over the months and years that many processes include a lot of retraced steps as work-in-progress moves first this way and then that.

Not long ago I was in a service station in Belgium that illustrates this perfectly. Usually we find in self-service cafes that you walk along an orderly line starting by collecting your tray near the entrance, then moving past the starters counter and the main course selections before arriving at the desserts, drinks and finally arriving at the till, which is itself conveniently located near the tables. The service station I found myself in had me walking across the floor to the trays only to return for the starters. The main courses and desserts were lined up fine but unfortunately you ended up at the opposite end of the room to where you needed to pay. The drinks were located elsewhere.

Over time our workplaces can begin to show the same illogical arrangement as that service station, but as this can be a gradual process we hardly notice it until it is pointed out. Take a look at your departments and see if there is excessive walking or retracing of steps between one process and the next. Actually draw a floor diagram of your area indicating all the desks and equipment found there and then indicate the routes

87

taken by work as it travels the system. You may just be surprised. A simple diagram is given opposite as an example.

Therefore, the first step in improving flow is to line up processes around the plant in order. But what processes should we include in our reorganisation? Are all processes of equal value? That is what we also need to determine during the **Straighten** stage of 5S Kaizen. What are those activities that add value and what are those activities that detract from us adding value? Which activities help us to give customers what they want when they want it, and which do not?

To lessen lead-time and give us greater flexibility in meeting delivery dates, we need to remove all wasteful activities. A popular method for this is to congregate the team around a large sheet of decorator's lining paper and assign each with a pad of post-its. Each process from beginning to end is written on the pad and, if known, the time that activity takes. Before long you may find the sheet covered in post-its, and depending on the size of the department and the number of activities and processes that go on there, it can reach several metres long. Don't just focus on the physical production line but include the travel or flow of information if appropriate.

Once this map has been finished you can identify those activities that do not add value and when used in conjunction with the floor plan, you have a powerful method for improving the flow of work, slashing lead-times and keeping to agreed timescales for production.

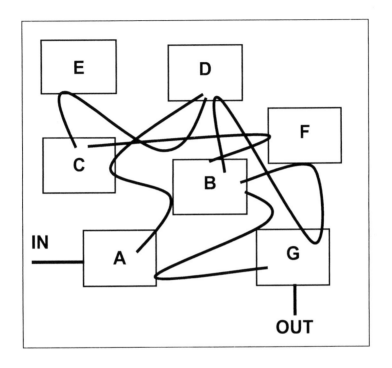

Replacing the necessary

Now you are on your way to an understanding of work flow, the value stream, and where activities are to be located in a logical and sequential order. You are also in a better position to know where those items that were the focus of the red-tagging exercise during **Sort**, should be returned to and how the items that remained should be organised.

Whatever is needed immediately should be within arm's reach and so reduce the waste of motion. This will also reduce the time wasted having to look for much needed items of equipment. All other items should be positioned according to their frequency of use. Remember when we moved unnecessary furniture and equipment in the red-tag area? Do you also remember how the sample tag indicated the date? This was the reason, to allow the level of usage to be determined. Those things we use rarely can be placed furthest away and probably stored in a cupboard or room. We can justify a short walk for something we use only once a week but what we cannot justify is walking for everyday items.

Those tools that are used together should also be stored together and in the order of use. Once again, it is not uncommon to see people hunting at the back of a store cupboard or at the bottom of a toolbox trying to find what they are looking for. One method to help this is to make these storage areas bigger then usual so that things can be properly arranged and clearly seen.

Working to order

We may also want to consider at this stage how work assignments are carried out. A useful feature of this is to begin seeing our processes as a kind of supplier/customer relationship. As it is our intention always to please the customer, then the operator of process A should be working to satisfy and please process B and so on. This means providing the next process downstream to us with exactly what they need when they need it. Usually we put a machine to work, and while it is set up for a particular job we get it to produce as many parts as possible, regardless of the amount actually needed by the next process. This is the traditional way of working and is termed a **push** system, as workloads are physically pushed from the back through the production cycle. It is also more commonly called a batch-and-queue model as work is carried out in large batches and then queued along the conveyor until the internal customer is ready for them.

In 'lean' organisations, operations follow a **pull** system in that the processes pull work downstream. When process B requires more work, then a visible symbol known as a **kanban** is given telling the operator above when to deliver more work and in what quantities. To understand a kanban better it may be useful to know that many of us already use them on a daily basis. Think of what you do when you put the empty milk bottles out at night. You are visibly signally to the milkman that you require another pint of milk. On seeing the empty bottle, the kanban, he gets to work by replacing the empty bottle with the full. In a similar way, work should only be carried out in the amounts needed and to order. Another name for the pull system is **'just-in-time'** (JIT) and was developed by Taiichi Ohno at Toyota. Using this method helps reduce the amounts of work-in-progress and the waiting time between processes.

Careful time management is needed for this to run smoothly and the work to flow, but the savings are enormous when compared to the older method.

Action Plan

- Straighten is very much the 're-engineering' stage of 5S Kaizen where every activity within the department is broken down into its constituent parts and reorganised so as to improve efficiency and productivity as well as the overall flow of work being carried out.

- Collect the team around a large sheet of decorator's lining paper and hand out 'post-it' pads to each individual.

- Ask them to walk the system and write down on separate 'post-its' each and every activity including were possible the total time to complete each process.

- Draw a simple floor plan of the department, including the locations of equipment and furniture, and indicate the movement of work as it travels round the various processes.

- Use the floor plan and process map you have created to identify wasteful activities that do not add value, and any retracing of steps and bottlenecks that hinder flow.

- Remove all repeated steps and non-value adding activities.

- Develop ideas about how to invest less in those activities that do not add value but are still necessary in a supportive role.

- Where possible relocate equipment and furniture to aid flow.

- Locate those items left in place after the Sort exercise in more appropriate positions, preferably within arms length of the operative.

- Red Tagged items should be screened as to frequency of use and returned to the work area at suitable distances from the workplace.

- Apply visual management controls throughout the department including marking walkways around the department, placing identifying signs on the doors of rooms, and labelling storage cupboard doors with their contents.

- Label all shelving, listing the contents of each shelf and bay.

- Think of ways with the team to begin a just-in-time and kanban system to remove excessive stock.

- Look for opportunities to apply poke-yoke techniques to reduce defects and implement a zero-defects or 'right first time' approach to production.

6

Shine

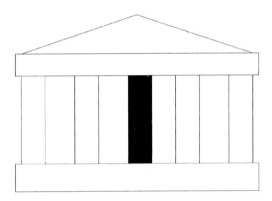

We now have a very orderly and airy environment in which to work. However, is it a clean environment? That is the purpose of **Shine** – to ensure that the area remains clean and tidy at all time.

Shine is probably the only step that can begin as the previous stage is still running. Why place the much-needed equipment back into your immediate vicinity if it is dirty? Instead, as items are being designated new locations, both the locations and the items need to be cleaned before returning. That's common sense.

But **Shine** is about more than just keeping everything clean,

Shine also deals with maintaining our equipment in top working condition. This removes the waste incurred through faulty equipment and costly repairs. Usually we tend to think of such a thorough cleaning and maintenance in terms of yearly events, the 'spring clean' for example, but in 5S Kaizen, such attention to cleanliness and keeping equipment in optimal working condition should be an on going daily concern.

When we are at home it is easy to let the junk pile up. I'm sure we have all at one time or another felt the frustration of living in a cluttered environment and have experienced the relief when we knuckle down and do something about it. Such a feeling is the same when we practice **Shine** in our places of work. Hence we can find after implementing the first three steps of 5S Kaizen that our spirits are lifted, and we can concentrate more on our tasks, free as we are from the frustration of working in dirty or cluttered surrounding with faulty, or imperfect equipment.

Lifting morale

I have worked in many factories that could benefit enormously from such a systematic cleaning exercise. The working areas were anything but clean, and often workers' clothes at the end of their shifts were black with dust and grime picked up from the environment. If you wonder how clean your department really is, one way to tell is to look at the cleanliness of your workers as they leave the plant at night.

Working in dirty or unclean conditions does little for staff morale. Windows covered in soot and grime obscure daylight from entering the building, which scientists say is important for psychological well-being. Also, the potential for serious accidents occurring is greater in such environments where dirty floors obscure any traces of spilt oil or grease which others can slip on. One common example of dirty (and dangerous) environments is machines with broken safety guards or those with see-through guards which are so dirty they are practically useless. All this has an effect on morale and safety yet can be improved by simply keeping on top of house keeping responsibilities.

A short while ago I received an email from someone at Fujitsu. He was writing to me after reading an article I published about the 5S Kaizen approach. An interesting point he made was that the **Shine** stage is all about reducing the need for a complete and thorough cleaning program in the future and he's right. Every worker should be held responsible for their areas, even if it means finishing ten or fifteen minutes earlier to work on housekeeping. In plants were a shift system operates such cleanliness is a real necessity if you want the second operative to begin work straight away. Nothing can be more frustrating than leaving your area clean for the next person only to find on your return the place looking a tip with oily rags, grease and various tools carelessly and randomly left about the place. Following the steps of **Shine**, as well as those in the previous **Straighten** stage, helps eliminate these problems and raise morale.

Inspecting cleanliness

As mentioned previously, besides just being a cleaning exercise **Shine** is also about inspecting our working environments and checking that everything is in optimal condition for work. This is an approach we term '**total productive maintenance**' or TPM.

TPM began in the plants of Nippon Densho, a supplier of parts to Toyota. At its heart it is a standardised method of inspecting equipment to ensure it is able to meet the necessary work quotas to meet their clients' specifications. TPM is all about ongoing inspection and observation by the operator. This has been shown to raise quality standards by reducing the number of defects created by that machine. Imagine you work on a press with a blade that over time becomes loose. There is an increasing risk that the longer the machine works, the more defects it will produce due to either the loosening or blunting of the blade. Under TPM such a condition would be noted and written into the standard for that operation, as well as accounted for when calculating that machine's daily output; moreover, under the TPM procedures, the machine would be inspected for five minutes every hour (or as often as deemed necessary) and any loosening bolts tightened and blunt blades replaced by the operative. This very simple step would ensure that the machine was always working at optimal capacity and ensure there were no defects created due to this problem.

Because of practising **Shine** as part of a 5S Kaizen program, many companies have found their corporate image increase as well as their sense of professionalism. Their guarantees towards quality assurance and meeting targets are no longer carefully crafted words on a page but are demonstrated everyday on the shopfloor, which is now so clean that they are able to use it as an extension to their showroom.

Implementing Shine

As mentioned earlier, **Shine** can begin during the **Straighten** stage. However, a method of continuous inspection and cleaning must be developed to keep on top of things. We do not want to fall into the trap of getting everything shipshape during this program only to find it dirty again after a few weeks or months. We should not become complacent in our approach to cleanliness and only apply **Shine** when things are getting too bad.

According to Hiroyuki Hirano it is worthwhile thinking of our workplace in terms of three criteria or categories. These are:

- Workplace storage or warehouse
- Equipment
- Estates.

The first of these covers items that are held in storage such as raw materials in the goods-in department and work-in-progress stored on pallets around the factory (though hopefully these will be at a minimum if we implemented just-in-time and pull systems during **Straighten**). 'Equipment' is as its name suggests and includes items of furniture, computers and printers, as well as the general tools we find in the workshop. Finally, 'estates', or 'space' as it is sometimes translated, refers to floors and walls, notice boards, cupboards, and walkways, which should be clearly marked out.

Each person must be made responsible for his or her immediate environment and for maintaining the cleanliness of the above three categories. The boundaries of each area can be indicated and displayed on a board. The floor plan we created during **Straighten** is ideal for working out who has responsibility for which area. Obviously if an operator moves around the area department and changes duties with each move, then his cleaning duties and responsibilities will change with each move.

Then, at the end of each shift or day, a certain amount of time should be allocated for **Shine** activities including the cleaning and returning of all equipment to their rightful place, cleaning and inspecting the machinery we have been using and making sure the floor and walls are clean and free from any spillages or shavings. If the area includes a notice board then one should also check that all the postings are relevant and in date, and any notice that has passed its expiry date or is no longer necessary can be discarded, or kept in a nearby place until you can determine whether or not it should be replaced (a little bit like the red-tag areas). Any work-in-progress should also be properly stored or packaged if not being used until the next day, to avoid any damage. And finally, nothing must be left in the walkways.

Besides setting aside a period of time at the end of each day we must also try hard to maintain the **Shine** standard throughout the day. If anyone spills oil or grease on the floor they must clean it immediately and not wait until the assigned period before doing so. In this way the actual time needed at the end of the shift or day will be minimal and hence we often hear it referred to as the '**5 minute shine**' event.

Action Plan

Shine is about cleaning and inspecting the work area. Though it is primarily concerned with improving the physical environment it can also help the psychology of the work place by boosting staff morale and improving corporate culture and self-image.

- Shine can be started during the Straighten stage when red-tagged items are relocated around the department.

- Assign each operative in the department with an area they are responsible for. This can be drawn on the 5S map we created earlier.

- In departments with a rotational duty roster each activity should be assigned an area that the operative will be responsible for.

- Introduce staff to Hirano's three Shine categories: storage/warehouse, equipment and estates or space. For each activity area or person, draw up a list of the items under these categories which they will be responsible for in that area.

- Implement a daily 'Shine Time', usually at the end of a shift or the end of the day.

- **Remember that Shine is about inspection as well as cleaning**

- **Those members of staff who need training in basic machine maintenance should be enrolled onto a course or should receive training in-house.**

$\overline{\underline{\overline{7}}}$

Standardise

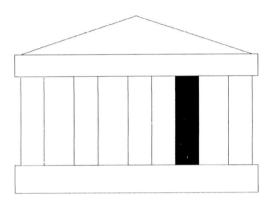

We now come to the stage of the 5S Kaizen method where those areas we have improved need to become the standard. When we think of a standard it is usual to think of a rule, or a guideline, that shows us the way we are to go and the path we are to keep to. The step **Standardise** enables us to apply techniques that help us to keep our work areas as shrines to efficiency.

> *A Standard Definition:*
>
> **'A standard is a published specification that establishes a common language and contains a technical specification or other precise criteria and is designed to be used consistently, as a rule, a guideline, or a definition.'**
> **British Standards Institute (BSI)**

Standardise along with the next step, **Sustain,** is also the start of embedding the 5S Kaizen approach to workplace improvement into your department or company's culture. As the illustration below will show, **Standardise** and **Sustain** work together at a deeper level than the first three levels which are mostly operational and highly visual.

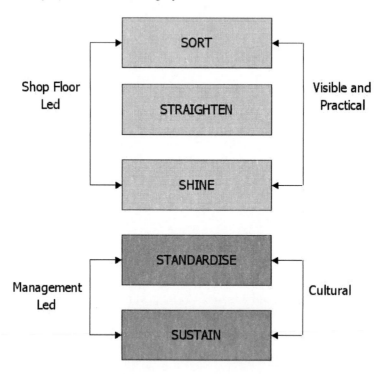

As the diagram shows, whereas the first three steps were very much concentrated on the procedural aspects of the job and the physical environment, **Standardise** looks more to how to manage the continuous application of 5S Kaizen. Hence the lead in this area tends to come from management rather than the staff members who make up the actioning teams of the previous steps.

That is not to say that our teams are not involved. Quite the contrary, for it is from staff that many of the new ways of working that make up the standard for that activity will come. Rather, it is management's responsibility that those standards are maintained and updated regularly. Also it is their responsibility to ensure that the standards become almost second nature to the workforce so that over time they will influence the cultural levels of our places of work and become the norm, the way we do things around here. Once this cultural level has been influenced enough, the standards will then be taught and passed on to new recruits.

Edgar Schein, a guru of organisational behaviour, has spent many decades studying and understanding organisational culture. His model described in the book *Organisational Culture and Leadership* presents us with a three-tier hierarchy arranged in order of visibility. The first tier is associated with organisational climate, or what he terms the cultural artefacts of an organisation, meaning those elements of corporate society that are visible and easily identified and measured. Cultural artefacts include behavioural norms, the language used and the visible symbols of a company, including the physical architecture. The myths and legends of an organisation that have built up over time, and which are verbally passed down to new recruits, are also an example of a company's cultural artefacts.

Below this level lies the organisation's values and espoused beliefs that are evidenced via such things as a company's mission statement, objectives and departmental policies and operating procedures. These espoused beliefs are a reflection of the learned responses that have developed over time through the shared experience of group members as the organisation has grown and dealt with various internal and external pressures. According to Schein, espoused values and beliefs 'constitute the basic foundations for making judgements and distinguishing "right" from "wrong" behaviour' and as such can be temporary in nature and only held until another solution becomes known or the current practice fails to deliver its promised results. Once the espoused belief or value loses its validity it is quickly replaced by another competing view of what is right.

The lowest level of Schein's model is the level of unconscious assumptions. This level refers to the invisible taken-for-granted truths of the company. Through repetition, organisations have developed solutions that have worked and thereby provided them with reliable and repeatable outcomes that reinforce the espoused belief of what is the right course of action in any given situation. 'When a solution to a problem works repeatedly, it comes to be taken for granted. What was once a hypothesised hunch or value gradually comes to be treated as a reality. We come to believe that nature really works this way.' Whereas espoused beliefs and values expressed a commonly held view of how things should be, unconscious assumptions express how something is and therefore presumes that there is no other alternative; unconscious assumptions are non-debatable. Schein therefore describes culture thus:

> 'The culture of a group can now be defined as a pattern of shared basic assumptions that was learned by a group as it solved its problems of external adaptation and internal integration, that has worked well enough to be considered valid and, therefore, to be taught to new members as the correct way to perceive, think, and feel in relation to those problems.'

This model sits well with the 5S Kaizen ladder shown above. In the first three steps of **Sort**, **Straighten** and **Shine** we dealt very much with the visible artefacts of the organisation or department – how things look and feel. **Standardise**, the point where we are now, looks at the way things happen, the espoused beliefs as evidenced by policies and procedures, with **Sustain**, which we will cover in the next chapter, focusing on ingraining this approach into our culture so that it becomes an almost unconscious and 'taken for granted' reality.

Why Standardise?

The standardisation of tasks is the first-line defense against old ways of working and old habits resurfacing. It is natural for humans to revert back to what they know best in times of change and by standardising the activities of each process helps us to safeguard against this undesirable trait.

These habits include not being too particular with regard to tidying up, and keeping on top of equipment maintenance duties. As the weeks pass, the workplace starts to look more like what it used to look like rather than what it should look like. Also, we start raiding the stationary cupboard again as soon as a new delivery arrives. I've never understood why that happens but it does. As soon as new pads, pens and jotters appear in the cupboard there is a mad rush to claim as many as we possibly can.

Standardisation helps consolidate the activities of the previous steps and presents them as a whole. It helps us to manage ongoing improvements and to see were we are against our objectives. Set out on page 112 is a list of nine reasons or benefits of standardisation that was drawn up by Masaaki Imai for his book *Gemba Kaizen – A Common Sense, Low Cost Approach to Management.*

Before I begin to explain how to apply **Standardise** there is one point I would like to make. Many people see standards as immovable, as if set in stone. They see the standard as the central pillar that is stable and solid. In 5S Kaizen, however, standards are fluid and dynamic. They constantly change over time, maybe even daily on occasions. As workers develop better ways of working and feed these back to management, this becomes the new standard and remains so until another improvement suggestion is applied and found to be valid. To repeat Schein who we quoted above, these standards 'can be temporary in nature and only held until another solution becomes known or the current practice fails to deliver its promised results. Once the espoused belief or value loses its validity it is quickly replaced by another competing view of what is right.'

Benefits of Standardisation

1. Standardisation represents the best, easiest, and safest way to do a job.

2. It offers the best way to preserve know-how and expertise.

3. It provides a way to measure performance.

4. It shows relationships between cause and effect.

5. It provides a basis for maintenance and improvement.

6. It provides objectives and indicate training - goals.

7. It provides a basis for training.

8. It creates a basis for audit or diagnosis.

9. It provides a means for preventing the reoccurrence of errors and for minimising variability.

Implementing standards

A good way to apply standards is through a regular auditing system. These audits cover all the five steps but mainly concentrate on the first three 'active' levels, **Sort**, **Straighten** and **Shine**, and on monitoring the maintenance schedule. The audits should be a regular part of our work and held on a monthly basis. Anything over a month would be pointless as a standardising method and many companies schedule weekly audits so as to constantly keep on top of problems and slipping standards as they occur, and keep the 5S Kaizen philosophy firmly in people's minds.

The 5S Kaizen audit, as with any auditing system, requires designing a check sheet that asks pertinent questions regarding the application of the five steps. An example audit sheet is shown on the next two pages and there are two approaches we can use when conducting an audit.

The first scores each question as to the level of conformance. These are usually along the lines of a Lickertt scale where each number corresponds to the level of compliance. For example:

- Poor
- Average
- Good
- Excellent

This was the way I had always conducted 5S Kaizen audits in the past but recently I was talking to an experienced Kaizen facilitator who recommended a more binary approach, i.e.: design the questionnaire so that a simple 'yes,' or 'no' could be provided as an answer. Using the Lickertt scale allows for a subjective response, and depending on who is responsible for

My Company International
5S Kaizen Audit

Auditor ....
Date ....
Dept. ....
Manager ....

Yes = 1   No = 0

SORT	Y/N
1. Have all unnecessary items been removed?	
2. Are red tags in use throughout the department?	
3. Are all notice boards up to date?	
4. Are there any red tags more than 4 weeks old?	
5. Is all equipment/WIP not in use correctly stored away?	
Score	

STRAIGHTEN	Y/N
1. Are all walkways clearly marked out?	
2. Are the separate work sections clearly identifiable?	
3. Are all storage areas (shelves/cupboards etc.) labeled?	
4. Is all needed work loads in their proper place?	
5. Is the workplace arranged orderly to improve flow?	
Score	

SHINE	Y/N
1. Are all walkways free from clutter?	
2. Are all walls, floors and work areas free from dirt?	
3. Is all equipment regularly maintained and cleaned?	
4. Is there a regular cleaning routine?	
5. Is everyone involved in cleaning duties?	
Score	

Page 1

My Company International
5S Kaizen Audit

Date ....

STANDARDISE	Y/N
1. Are there regular 5S audits?	
2. Is there an SOP for each activity?	
3. Are the SOP's reviewed and updated regularly?	
4. Is everyone trained according to the latest SOP?	
5. Are the results of 5S audits prominently displayed?	
Score	

SUSTAIN	Y/N
1. Is there a staff suggestion system in place?	
2. Are the suggestions being reviewed and actioned?	
3. Are the audits being reviewed and actioned?	
4. Is there a regular team meeting?	
5. Has the area been accredited?	
Score	
Total Score	

Signed by Auditor ....

Signed by Manager ....

Audit Reviewed On ....

Please use the reverse side for additional comments.

conducting the audit that week or month, a different score could be produced. Rather than the score reflecting what actually is, it would be nothing more than a reflection of what the auditor believes it to be.   In other words there would be no standardisation of the auditing process.   Answering a simple 'yes it does' or 'no it doesn't' check sheet removes any subjective interpretation of the environment and supplies a more consistent and objective set of results.

After the audit is complete and correctly scored, the results should be displayed to all and discussed at the morning Prep Talk (see the next chapter). A 'radar chart', which represents scores in a multiple-axis diagram (see example below), is ideal for this as it shows in a very pictorial fashion where improvement has occurred and more importantly where there is room for improvement. By adding to the same chart over the coming months a picture of overall improvement can be plotted and compared. To make it even more visual and easy to read, each month's score can be recorded in a different colour.

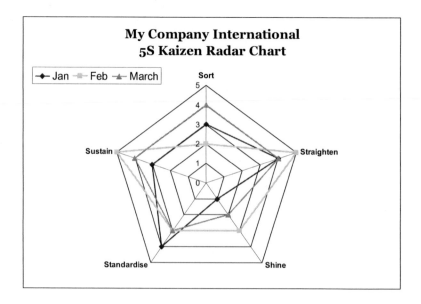

The audit should also include monitoring maintenance times and checking whether or not maintenance has been regularly carried out. For this to happen, each operative should make a log of checks recording the time and any corrective outcome if applicable. A simple form will suffice that is attached to the machine and which can be checked during the audit (see overleaf). When complete, these sheets can be handed to management for filing and to ascertain if there are any reoccurring problems.

My Company International
TPM LOG SHEET

Name of Operator:...

Department:...

Machine/Equipment:..

Date of last check (from previous record):............................

Date	Time	Comments	Initials

Approved by:...

Picture perfect

Another way to improve standards is through the use of photographs. When we have completed the first three 5S steps we should photograph the work areas (the photographs thus acting as the 'standards') and place the photographs in prominent positions around the department. For example a machine-station photograph should be displayed at eye-level in front of the machine concerned. Then even while they are working, members of staff are reminded of the standard and how the area must be kept at all times.

Many companies also like to keep a 'before and after' photo diary. This is not only to motivate them to continue – do you really want it to go back to this? – but also to show to clients as they walk the plant so that they can see for themselves the improvements you have made.

These are just a few standardising suggestions for you to think about and apply. No doubt you will think of your own as you practice this method so that the improvements you realised will remain in place permanently. With this in mind then lets move on to **Sustain**, the last step of the 5S Kaizen way.

Action Plan

- Train and assign auditors of your area.

- Devise an regular auditing schedule with your auditors.

- Design audit questionnaires.

- Carry out the audits at least month a month.

- Take photographs of the environment after the first five steps are complete.

- Display these photographs in prominent positions around the department so all can see and be reminded of the standard.

- Design TPM log sheets and distribute.

- When auditing don't forget to also check the log sheets.

- Also check that appropriate reviews of the 5S Kaizen audits and TPM log sheets are being carried out.

8

Sustain

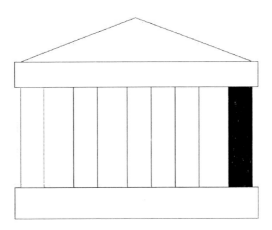

So here we are at the final stage of the 5S Kaizen program, but before we crack open the Champagne, a word of warning. Though this may very well be the last stage, it is also the one with no end and often regarded as the hardest to implement.

Imagine if all the hard work you put into the previous four steps was for nothing. Imagine if all the benefits you realised and the potential for improvement you identified was to remain unrealised. Well, unless you take a firm hold of this final step and implement the methods and techniques outlined here, that is exactly what will happen.

These are not idle threats. It has happened many times before, to many a well-intentioned company – they follow the first four steps; they encourage their staff to offer suggestions and even work hard at removing the waste and straightening the flow of work; but there it stops. Within months, the old processes and systems resurface and reclaim their dominant positions on the shop floor. Wasteful activities increase and deadlines for delivery dates begin to be missed. Quality drops and productivity slows as rejects clog the system. It has happened before, it is happening now and it will happen to you unless you keep on top of the activities and sustain the efforts you have made.

The consequences of failure at this stage can be serious. Staff morale falls back to an even lower level than before the start of the whole 5S process. Imagine for a moment how it must feel if you were a member of staff, fed up with the inefficiencies you see in the workplace yet feeling powerless to do anything about them. Then along comes a change champion who gives you the necessary training and responsibility to make those alterations and improve things. Imagine the strong sense of belonging to the company and of being valued by it, not to mention the motivation to continue each day doing your best knowing that your concerns will be listened to and acted on if necessary. Then let's imagine that suddenly, or even over time, you saw things slipping back to their former drudgery. Your improvement suggestions get pushed to the back and you find yourself being instructed, and in no uncertain terms, to 'just get on with things, you're paid to work!'

Kaizen, as you should well know by this stage, means continuous improvement, with the emphasis on *continuous*. In this chapter I will introduce you to methods that will help you sustain your efforts and ensure that your hard work has not been in vain. As before these tools have been tried and tested in many businesses in many sectors of industry and if you apply them, and keep on top of things, your continuous improvement will be just that and your business will go from strength to strength.

Another aspect of **Sustain** is that, though it may be the last step, it is also the springboard for the first in a continually repeating, continually refining cycle of organisational change. Although **Sustain** is the last step in this book and on the 5S Kaizen ladder, it does not mean that the previous four can be put to one side and forgotten about. This in fact is what differentiates the Western approach from the East. What we lay down here is a platform on which the other steps, on their second pass, will be based. Without **Sustain** it will all disintegrate and become dysfunctional. When questioned about his experiences implementing this method, Peter Carver of Clares Merchandise Handling Equipment Ltd had this to say regarding **Sustain**:

'This is by far the hardest. Keeping things going after they have been implemented is tough. People naturally fall back into their old ways if they are allowed to.'

Communicate!

The first step in the **Sustain** process is to appoint a communications officer. Depending on the size of your company the post doesn't need to be a full time role but it is vital to the **Sustain** program. If you are of a sufficient size and already have a communications officer then offering a part-time role to someone on the shop floor would also be a good idea and help to increase involvement in the project.

I know we talked about communication in chapter 3 but this is a little different. Back then, before we began our change campaign, we were communicating with the sole intent of selling the method, getting support at all levels of the business, identifying change agents we could work with and who could pass the message on and build up support and followers as though they were some kind of apostles for change. Now we are delivering another type of communication. People know the tools, they know the theory and depending on the extent and depth of your original campaign they may even know a few Japanese words. But now that message needs to focus more on the benefits already achieved, so as to convince any remaining doubters, and needs to be reaffirmed, strengthened and repeated every day so that 5S Kaizen is always on everyone's mind and eventually becomes the norm in your place of work.

There are a number of ways your communications officer can achieve this and none of them costs a great deal. One good method is to publish your own in-house 5S Kaizen newsletter. This can be self-published with any good desktop publishing software, Microsoft PowerPoint (don't forget to resize to A4 portrait), or even a word-processor. Ideally it should be attention-getting and shout '*read me*'. Not so much a heavy broadsheet as an information filled compact. It should be uplifting, positive and totally committed to sending out clear communications regarding your 5S vision.

The reason I say this is that unless such a commitment to the publication is strong, within a few editions it will become nothing more than a general newsletter filled with gossip, general expectations of future growth and a monthly chairman's letter saying how well we are all working and to keep it up. Within a few editions more it will be scrapped as a waste of time and company paper. The position of communications officer may well be deemed redundant and discontinued. The end result will be that without an effective means of communication, you can forget long-term continuous improvement and your change campaign will be finished.

Ideally the newsletter should appear on a regular basis, but to use it to its full effect I recommend a quarterly edition as being the ideal. It's not so frequent that it bores people or becomes difficult to fill; at the same time it's not so infrequent that the message will be forgotten. It should contain many snippets of Kaizen knowledge, as well as the main activity-based features, and in this respect will become another educational tool for you to use – and there will always be something to read!

The 5S Kaizen newsletter should regularly update employees of the change events planned and the successes realised. Photograph areas that have improved through 5S Kaizen activities and interview those who work there. Seeing their names and departments in print will lift morale and help them feel that their contribution was of value and worthwhile. They've actually done something positive to help the company.

The early morning prep

Aligned with your communication strategy should be the early morning prep talk. Many companies have found that as a means to motivate and thereby sustain change, speaking with staff in a group setting before the day's work commences brings great results. Usually these meetings focus on handing out assignments if a new rota is due and communicating the daily production requirements to meet targets.

Where problems have been found from the previous day, suggestions can be obtained there and then from the team, the ones 'in the know', and if realistic can be implemented that day. This allows for immediate action bringing with it a high level of flexibility and adaptation into the workplace.

Also a review of recent audit activity can be given pointing out where improvements have been realised and areas to focus on this period. Usually, these meetings are short and to the point followed by a hearty 'BANZAI!!!'

Whether your company's culture is one of air punching, americanised motivational techniques, or a more reserved and formal environment, the early morning prep talk can be adapted to suit. The talks are a great way to keep your staff informed of problems and targets and to help them to feel involved in the company's business.

Get writing

Previously I've referred to staff suggestion systems and how they provide us with a great tool for sustaining improvements. Nothing is more powerful to raise morale than the knowledge that our ideas and thoughts will be listened to and discussed honestly, and if they are found to be of use and implemented, then all the better.

However, as one of the pillars of 5S Kaizen is **Standardise**, it wouldn't do to just have 'old Joe' casually shouting out his thoughts as we pass, though he can if he wants and probably will anyway. With the prevalence of computers in the workplace let all suggestions be emailed to the necessary manager with the subject clearly stating 'SUGGESTION' and nothing else in capital letters so it will stand out in the inbox. Those on the shopfloor without access to a PC could post suggestions on paper, making clear the manager for whose attention it is and these suggestions can be delivered along with other internal post.

5S Kaizen School

Obviously for any suggestion to be meaningful and practical, members of staff must understand and have knowledge of 5S Kaizen and 'lean' principles. The type of suggestions we want are not the 'let's all finish an hour earlier', 'how about more holidays?' or 'my child really needs me at home by 3:30, I was wondering if...' type. Rather, what we need are suggestions that have some actual relevance to the work we do and how to improve the flow of work between processes and the value stream. The success of the suggestion system is directly related to the level of knowledge imparted around the company.

The newsletter mentioned above is one way to impart knowledge but I also suggest that a formal educational system is also set up. The training itself can consist of 'classroom' education to cover the theory and on-the-job practical work. Assignments can be issued where 5S Kaizen trainees and newly appointed members of staff, who by the way should attend the school early in their employment, can solve a production-based problem and write a report on their findings. By doing this, it is not only good for the individual, but their solutions would benefit the company itself and may even pay for the education.

At the beginning you may need to bring in a consultancy group to set up the training program, but once enough staff have been through the course, there is no reason not to use these newly skilled employees to deliver future training rather than the outside specialists. You could even (and I recommend this) prepare in-house certificates that the trainee's receive on successful completion of the course – another worthy item for the monthly newsletter.

5S Kaizen accreditations

In the last chapter we introduced the 5S Kaizen audit as a means to maintain, and thereby sustain, the workplace standards. By the very nature of having auditable standards, the introduction of accreditations is a natural progression. In addition to training staff in the 5S Kaizen way and appointing 5S Kaizen auditors, offering certification as a way to acknowledge departmental efforts is another easy to implement but highly effective means of sustaining interest.

Overleaf I have prepared a sample certificate you may use to model your own in-house accreditation award. These can be awarded after scoring highly on the audit over a set period of months.

My Company International

5S
Kaizen

Accreditation
Award

Presented to

The Goods In Department

For their commitment to continuous
workplace improvement

Presented On
25 – 10 – 2007

Award celebrations

Every year, or sooner if you wish, try holding an award ceremony for those who have been spotted to be making an extra effort to improve. If your company is small enough you could invite everyone. To make the event memorable and to ensure it is talked about afterwards at work and looked forward to, hold the ceremony off-site at a business function room or in a restaurant that will allow you to make the presentations. Put on some food and drink. This will help people relax and enjoy the occasion as well as helping staff members who work in different departments (and therefore would not normally communicate on a day to day basis) to get to know each other. The presentations can and should be for individual persons and for departments with a special award for those who have been able to achieve the most from their 5S Kaizen activities over the year.

If managed and communicated properly, these award ceremonies can be a great way to sustain interest in improving. They can generate much interest and talk around the workplace and of course fit in well with and complement other tools associated with the **Sustain** stage of 5S Kaizen.

5S Kaizen inter-departmental challenges

Some companies have found that regular inter-departmental challenges are useful to keep the improvement momentum alive. These challenges, however, do not need a separate strategy to implement but can be seen as a natural by-product of the auditing system and the award celebrations. Using these tools, a healthy and friendly competition builds up where everyone wants to win the improvement award for that period.

Obviously one does have to stimulate interest and communicate the awards as something to be coveted but often, by effectively implementing the newsletter, award celebrations, accreditations and the Kaizen School, such a desire for recognition on an organisational scale can be developed.

Walking the walk, and talking the talk

Possibly the best way to gain sustained improvement is by walking the floor and encouraging staff as they go about their day-to-day business. Listen to people with ideas and if they are good tell them to email or post their suggestion for consideration. Actively motivate by showing your own commitment to the change, because without that, all the communication, publication and suggestions will not make a bit of difference nor stir into action those very people who will be responsible for the success of your change endeavour.

With that last thought in mind, I remember a factory where my father worked back in the 1970s before we had even heard the term Kaizen. The Chairman and owner use to walk the shopfloor every morning and talked to the people. There were nearly 1,000 people working there and the majority worked in a labouring capacity. He used to carry a bag of toffees with him and share them out and when he ran out of toffees (which was very quickly) he would, and remember this is the 1970s, light a cigarette and have a smoke with them as they worked. Everyone called him 'Uncle Jack'.

As a consequence there was a great family feeling associated with the place and through his activity everyone knew the latest gossip from other areas of the factory. I remember when I went in on school holidays the feeling of belonging and I was just a small school kid running round playing. And to think this was the chairman of a very successful, multi-million pound, privately owned business.

There's a good Kaizen lesson to be learnt there. Sadly 'Uncle Jack' died but his actions can still teach us something today.

Action Plan

- Develop a communication strategy designed to keep the 5S Kaizen way at the forefront of everyone's mind.

- Appoint a communications officer or an assistant if one already in post.

- Hold morning Prep Talks to communicate that day's targets and to review audits and ask for suggestions.

- Design and develop an in-house 5S Kaizen newsletter or book a regular column in an existing one.

- Implement a staff suggestion system and encourage your staff members to use it.

- Design a deliver a Kaizen School to educate your staff in the 5S Kaizen way. Award certificates to successful trainees.

- Implement 5S Kaizen Accreditations for those areas that regularly score high on the 5S Kaizen audit.

- Hold annual award celebrations as well as those at the end of a 5S Kaizen event.

- Arrange and promote friendly inter-department challenge to motivate all to take part.

- Walk the shop floor regularly and get to know your staff.

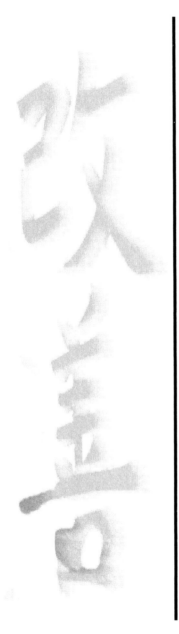

Conclusion

'To exist is to change, to change is to mature, to mature is to go on creating oneself endlessly.'

Henri Bergson

$$\overline{\underline{9}}$$

Looking Beyond the Day-to-Day

So there it is – the 5S Kaizen way towards total quality management and overall business improvement. With this method many companies have achieved success and I hope you have found this brief introduction of interest and you are looking forward to implementing some of the tools and techniques to your own work areas or even your company.

I mentioned in the introduction to this book that the world was changing at a hectic pace and that in order to satisfy our increasingly demanding customers we must develop ourselves into flexible and dynamic organisations. Fortunately I was not alone in this thought as John Kotter so apply puts in his book *Leading Change*:

> 'The rate of change in the business world is not going to slow down anytime soon. If anything, competition in most industries will probably speed up over the next few decades. Enterprises everywhere will be presented with even more terrible hazards and wonderful opportunities, driven by the globalisation of the economy along with related technological and social trends.'

Hopefully by applying the suggestions in this book you will find more opportunities than hazards in your journey as you constantly strive to become a high performance 21st century organisation.

What this approach is all about is teamwork: teaching people, even across disciplines and departments, to work together in solving problems. Usually people keep themselves to themselves, frightened to show any weaknesses or errors to the outside world. In this approach, they are encouraged to participate – and actively to communicate and discuss 'errors' so that they can be improved.

Working as teams also helps us integrate the layered hierarchies that are often found in large organisations and to develop an entrepreneurial approach to business. Managers' roles change from being fire-fighters, worrying each new day about the problems they will encounter, to becoming change leaders and motivators, encouraging staff to continually question and better themselves and their work each day. Sure there will always be the daily headaches but now you will have a department full of helpful advisors to assist you in finding a solution.

When you walk the floor each day you will get to know your staff better and help raise their morale. Your staff will feel valued by you and by the company and as such will be more willing to put in that little bit more effort.

In short 5S Kaizen, when applied properly, is a holistic approach to business success. Often thought of only in terms of bottom line results and procedural improvements, this approach to work improves all aspects of the company, both operationally and culturally. The question should not be 'should we try this?' but 'how can I afford not too?'.

Change is everywhere today and we must change also if we

are to stay in the game. Often though, tradition dictates and the changes never occur and the improvements are never realised. 5S Kaizen gives us the means, motivation and power to break free from stalled, historically bound ways of thinking and to release the shackles of the past as we raise ourselves to new heights. I hope you have enjoyed this book and wish you well in your future improvement endeavours. Remember, who we are today is what holds us back tomorrow.

Good luck in your change.

Recommended Reading

Hopefully, after my short introduction to the 5S Kaizen way towards business improvement, I have whetted your appetite and you now wish to learn some more. Here are some excellent reads that I recommend for your continued education into continuous improvement. Some of them are books I used when first learning of this approach; others I discovered whilst researching for this book.

Creating a Lean Culture: Tools to Sustain Lean Conversions (2005) David Mann, Productivity Press

Five Pillars of the Visible Workplace: The Source Book for 5S Implementation (1995) Hiroyuki Hirano, Productivity Press

Gemba Kaizen (1997) Massaki Imai, McGraw-Hill/Irwin

Hoshin Kanri: Policy Deployment for Successful TQM (2004) Yoji Akao, Productivity Press

Hoshin Kanri for the Lean Enterprise: Developing Competitive Capabilities And Managing Profit (2006) Thomas Jackson, Productivity Press

Inside the Mind of Toyota (2005) Satashi Hino and Jeff Liker, Productivity Press

Kaizen: the Key to Japan's Competitive Success (1986) Masaaki Imai, McGraw-Hill/Irwin

Lean Thinking (2003) James Womac and Daniel Jones, Free Press

The Elegant Solution: Toyota's Formula for Mastering Innovation (2006) Matthew May, Free Press

The Machine That Changed the World (1991) James Womac and Daniel Jones, Harper Perennial

The Toyota Way (2004) Jeff Liker, McGraw-Hill Education

The Toyota Way Field Book (2007) Jeff Liker and David Meier, McGraw-Hill Publishing

Taiichi Ohno's Workplace Management (2007) Taiichi Ohno, Gemba Press

Toyota Production System – Beyond Large-Scale Production (1988) Taiichi Ohno, Productivity Press